What people are s…

For a Ruthless Critique of All That Exists

Against the vogue retreat from critique and ecstatic embrace of the immanent, Tally offers a bounding defense of the mutual project of critique and literature to depart from the given world to make better social orders, compellingly insisting on that project's imaginative quality and its many joys.
Anna Kornbluh, University of Illinois at Chicago, author of *The Order of Forms: Realism, Formalism, and Social Space*

Over and against the caricature promulgated by "postcritiquers," according to which critique is inherently at odds with the literary text, Tally demonstrates how true critique works not only to draw out and complement the utopian dimension of literature—its crucial role in helping us to imagine new and better worlds—but to advance it as well. The result is a far more accurate and robust understanding of critique as a praxis that is fundamentally generative rather than destructive, committed rather than disinterested, joyous rather than dour. *For a Ruthless Critique of All That Exists* so ruthlessly sets the record straight on the continued importance—indeed, the indispensability—of critique that the next time one hears it averred that "critique has run out of steam," their immediate reply should be, "Wait, haven't you read Tally's book?!"
Russell Sbriglia, Seton Hall University, editor (with Slavoj Žižek) of *Subject Lessons: Hegel, Lacan, and the Future of Materialism*

Also by the Author

Topophrenia: Place, Narrative, and the Spatial Imagination. Indiana University Press, 2019. [9780253037664]

Fredric Jameson: The Project of Dialectical Criticism. Pluto Press,

2014. [9780745332109]

Poe and the Subversion of American Literature: Satire, Fantasy, Critique. Bloomsbury, 2014. [9781501309298]

Spatiality. The New Critical Idiom. Routledge, 2013. [9780415664400]

Utopia in the Age of Globalization: Space, Representation, and the World System. Palgrave Macmillan, 2013. [9780230391895]

Kurt Vonnegut and the American Novel: A Postmodern Iconography. Bloomsbury, 2011. [9781472507006]

Melville, Mapping and Globalization: Literary Cartography in the American Baroque Writer. Continuum Books, 2009. [9781441163219]

Edited Collections

Spatial Literary Studies: Interdisciplinary Approaches to Space, Geography, and the Imagination. Routledge, 2021. [9780367520106]

Teaching Space, Place, and Literature. Routledge, 2018. [9781138047037]

The Routledge Handbook of Literature and Space. Routledge, 2017. [9781138816350]

Ecocriticism and Geocriticism: Overlapping Territories in Environmental and Spatial Literary Studies (with Christine M. Battista). Palgrave Macmillan, 2016. [9781349559145]

The Geocritical Legacies of Edward W. Said: Spatiality, Critical Humanism, and Comparative Literature. Palgrave Macmillan, 2015. [9781349504268]

Literary Cartographies: Spatiality, Representation, and Narrative. Palgrave Macmillan, 2014. [9781349687527]

Kurt Vonnegut: Critical Insights. Salem Press, 2013. [9781429838320]

Geocritical Explorations: Space, Place, and Mapping in Literary and Cultural Studies. Palgrave Macmillan, 2011. [9781349298884]

For a Ruthless Critique of All That Exists

Literature in an Era of Capitalist Realism

For a Ruthless Critique of All That Exists

Literature in an Era of Capitalist Realism

Robert T. Tally Jr.

zer0 books

Winchester, UK
Washington, USA

JOHN HUNT PUBLISHING

First published by Zero Books, 2022
Zero Books is an imprint of John Hunt Publishing Ltd., No. 3 East St., Alresford,
Hampshire SO24 9EE, UK
office@jhpbooks.com
www.johnhuntpublishing.com
www.zero-books.net

For distributor details and how to order please visit the 'Ordering' section on our website.

ISBN: 978 1 78904 854 4
978 1 78904 855 1 (ebook)
Library of Congress Control Number: 2021938948

A CIP catalogue record for this book is available from the British Library.

Design: Stuart Davies

UK: Printed and bound by CPI Group (UK) Ltd, Croydon, CR0 4YY
Printed in North America by CPI GPS partners

Contents

For Fredric Jameson

Tu se' lo mio maestro e 'l mio autore

Sapere aude!
Immanuel Kant, quoting Horace

Critique has torn the imaginary flowers from the chain not in order that man shall continue to bear that chain without fantasy or consolation, but so that he shall throw off the chain and pluck the living flower.
Karl Marx

Doing our best is no longer good enough. We must now do the seemingly impossible.
Greta Thunberg

Acknowledgments

This book emerges from conversations with far too many friends and colleagues to name here, but suffice it to say that whatever utopian impulse animates this critique, which is also a celebration *of* critique, is empowered by the energetic commitment of so many brilliant students, teachers, and critics today. A number of the thoughts and some of the words that appear here were first presented at sessions of the Modern Language Association's and the American Comparative Literature Association's conferences, as well as at the Winter Theory Institute of the Society for Critical Exchange and as a guest lecturer at Shanghai Jiao Tong University, and I am very grateful to the organizers, fellow panelists, and audiences for their hospitality and constructive criticism. Early versions of some of this material have been published in *The Ideology Issue*, a special issue of *South Atlantic Quarterly*, Vol. 119, iss. 4 (October 2020), edited by Andrew Cole, *What's Wrong with Antitheory?* edited by Jeffrey Di Leo (Bloomsbury, 2020), and *symplokē*, Vol. 27, no. 1–2 (2019). In addition to Andrew and Jeffrey, I would like to especially thank Anna Kornbluh for her always revelatory thinking on these matters and her endless generosity to students, colleagues, and comrades everywhere. I should also mention Jonathan Arac, Christopher Breu, Paul A. Bové, Caroline Edwards, Ying Fang, Youngmin Kim, Melody Yunzi Li, Whitney May, Sianne Ngai, Daniel T. O'Hara, Ato Quayson, Bruce Robbins, Russell Sbriglia, Biwu Shang, Hortense Spillers, Kenneth Surin, Janelle Watson, Phillip E. Wegner, and Rob Sean Wilson, who have all generously provided insightful comments and enthusiastic support. This book is dedicated to Fredric Jameson, whom I first encountered over 30 years ago as my instructor in an introductory undergraduate course called "What is Literature?" and who remains a teacher of, and role model for, not only the best of what criticism has to offer today, but also the best of what it must strive to do in the future. And, as always, Reiko Graham makes the world a better place.

Introduction

"The Art of Voluntary Insubordination"

Contrary to the image painted by its opponents today, critique is a thoroughly joyous activity, one that is often inspired by a deeply felt love for the work and for the fields in which such work takes place. That a literary critic should love both literature and criticism ought to be obvious, and it should be equally obvious that such love would not be expressed in unthinking praise or narcissistic enjoyment, but through the real pleasure of careful reading, considered meditation, and creative speculation, or, in a word, *critique*.

I have often thought that this intense love of literature derives from the capacity of literary works of art to spark, empower, and expand the imagination. Reading itself is an imaginative activity, but literature—however we might choose to define this notoriously capacious and dynamic term—in a sense *belongs to* the imagination. Not that the human mind can be so easily divided into faculties or that various activities can be limits to such faculties' exclusive borders, but it may well be that (to borrow a sort of Kantian schema) literature partakes of the imagination in the ways that, say, logic appeals to the understanding or music to the emotions. As Northrop Frye argued, the study of literature is principally a means by which we can *educate* the imagination. By "educating the imagination," Frye also meant we could empower and employ the imagination to make our lives and our world better, resisting the stultifying effects of governments and the marketplace, for instance, to affirm our collective and individual freedom. The critic, in this sense, is engaged in an effort to illuminate, draw out, and extend the literary work's powers as a means of strengthening our own imaginations. The critic's enemy is thus any who would attempt to limit that imagination, and in particular, the enemy is any who would undermine literature's capacity for or effectiveness in empowering the imagination.

Critique therefore has a fundamentally political vocation: it is called to challenge the forces of the *status quo*, to oppose the tyranny of "what is" and to seek out potential alternatives. In his 1978 lecture "What is Critique?," Michel Foucault draws upon his reading of Kant and his meditations on the interrelations of power and knowledge in concluding that critique be understood as "the art of voluntary insubordination" (47). He notes that "there is something in critique which is akin to virtue," while also averring that "the critical attitude," as he calls it, ought to be viewed "as virtue in general" (43). This association between critique as a virtue and critique as an art emphasizes the degree to which Foucault imagines critical work as an active engagement with the world, and not at all an indolent or smug practice by one who sits back and makes judgmental pronouncements from afar, or whatever similar stereotype today's "postcritical" critics like to picture. The critic is not voluntarily insubordinate to the literary text in question, but rather to the structural or institutional forces governing one's ability to read and to think. The critic is neither paranoid nor anarchic, but focused on the precise situation and circumstances of the moment. Foucault states that the origin and motive of the critical attitude can be found, not in the question, "how not to be governed?" in the absolute sense of no government "at all," but rather in the question, "how not to be governed *like that*, by that, in the name of those principles, with such and such an objective in mind and by means of such procedures, not like that, not for that, not by them" (44). Critique is thus social as well as political, located within the social sphere, even as its practitioners may operate and discrete examples may take place in more limited spaces, including the space of the text.

For a Ruthless Critique of All That Exists: Literature in an Era of

Capitalist Realism takes as its point of departure two significant and, I argue, interrelated phenomena that have become increasingly salient in the twenty-first century. The first is the pervasive sense of what Mark Fisher had called "capitalist realism," in which—to cite the famous expression variously attributed to Fredric Jameson and Slavoj Žižek—it is easier to imagine the end of the world than the end of capitalism. Making reference to these theorists, Fisher defines *capitalist realism* as "the widespread sense that not only is capitalism the only viable political and economic system, but also that it is impossible even to *imagine* a coherent alternative to it" (2). As Fisher's emphasis suggests, and as Jameson in particular had pointed out in *The Seeds of Time*, "perhaps this is due to some weakness in our imaginations" (xii). The attenuation of the imaginative function in cultural criticism has far-reaching implications for the organization and reformation of institutions more generally. This manifests itself as a waning of speculative or theoretical energy, which in turn leads to a general capitulation to the tyranny of the actual, a tacit acceptance of the currently existing state of affairs, and the preemptive disavowal of alternative possibilities.

Connected to this is the second phenomenon: the prevalent tendency in literary and cultural criticism over the past 30 years or more to eschew critical theory and even critique itself, while championing approaches to cultural study that emphasize surface reading, thin description, ordinary language philosophy, object-oriented ontology, and postcritique. Together these forms of anticritical and antitheoretical criticism have constituted a tendency identified by Jeffrey J. Williams as "the new modesty" in literary studies, a tendency that has in its various incarnations come to dominate the humanities and other areas of higher education in recent years. Along with many other critics of these postcritical approaches, I maintain that the latter phenomenon within the spheres of higher education and literary studies has served to reinforce the former—that is, the iron cage of capitalist realism—with its much more extensive effects across the social body and in critical thinking *tout court*. The result has been to align literary and cultural criticism with the broad-based forces of neoliberalism whose influence has so deleteriously transformed not only higher education but the whole of society at large. I argue that, contrary to these trends, the time is ripe for "a ruthless critique of all that exists," to borrow a phrase from the young Marx. This book is thus intended as a provocation, at once a polemic and a call to action for literary and cultural critics, with the hope that such action may help to excite and empower the imagination.

Cultural criticism represents only a limited sector, and of course literary criticism operates at an even more restricted zone of inquiry and experience, within the broader social space. I do not mean to suggest that the manifold problems we face today can be solved by academic literary critics reading or teaching literature differently, and the squabbles among different groups of literature professors hardly matter at all in the broader scheme of things. As such, despite appearances perhaps, I have little interest in the so-called "method wars"—to use its hashtag-friendly label, suited to the Twittersphere in which many of their skirmishes seem to be fought most vociferously—*per se*. The battles waged between the two camps, postcritical surface readers on the one hand and hermeneuticists of suspicion on the other, may well be the sort of academic tempest-in-a-teapot of which non-academics, or academic nonpartisans, are understandably dismissive if not blissfully unaware. But I do find that aspects of this intellectual conflict are symptomatic of, and perhaps even affiliated with, broader and more baleful trends within higher education, which are themselves reflected in troubling developments in the cultures and society of the United States (and elsewhere) today.

Within the narrower world of higher education, the problems

associated with literary criticism are insignificant compared with those of waning public and private funding, lack of vision and support among leaders, the neoliberal reorganization of institutional resources, a consumerist ethos that undermines student success, the deplorable use of contingent labor, the unethical treatment of faculty and staff, and the pervasive exploitation of precarity in general, right down to the willful endangerment of lives amid the global health and economic crises, just to name a few of the best known challenges. Amid these problems, the quarrels of a bunch of mostly tenured professors are unsurprisingly deemed by others to be lamentably parochial if not far worse, in bad taste and completely out of touch with the real disasters swirling about them. This is a fair criticism, and these matters will not be improved directly by having more critical reading or thinking alone; nor will they be improved by ignoring the material social, political, and economic forces that serve as the conditions for the continuing possibility of these outrages. But literature remains a crucial way in which humans make sense of, and give form to, the world and their experience of it. There are ways of seeing made available through literary works and related forms that can illuminate social processes that contribute to our ability both to imagine alternatives to our intolerable circumstances and to change those circumstances for the better. As such, all things considered, the approach to the study of literature matters.

When Karl Marx asserted the need for a ruthless critique of all that exists (*die rücksichtlose kritik alles bestehenden*) in an 1843 letter to Arnold Ruge, later published in the Deutsch-Französische Jahrbücher in February 1844, he did so in the context of criticizing not only the bourgeois society of the time but also the approaches of various radical or reformist movements, which Marx found wanting in their lack of vision for both the present and the future. But Marx also acknowledges that no blueprint of the future, post-capitalist society was possible or even desirable from vantage of the present situation, and this made it clear what *was* required of revolutionaries at the time: critique. As he explained,

> The internal difficulties seem to be almost greater than the external obstacles. For even though the question "Whence?" presents no problems, the question "Whither?" is a rich source of confusion. Not only has universal anarchy broken out among the reformers, but also every individual must admit to himself that he has no precise idea about what ought to happen. However, this very defect turns to the advantage of the new movement, for it means that we do not anticipate the world with our dogmas but instead attempt to discover the new world through the critique of the old...If we have no business with the construction of the future or with organizing it for all time, there can still be no doubt about the task confronting us at present: the ruthless criticism of the existing order, ruthless in that it will shrink neither from its own discoveries, nor from conflict with the powers that be. (*Early Writings*, 207)

If, in 1843, critics could not predict the future, today we are perhaps even far less equipped with such premonitory or speculative powers to descry as-yet-unimagined social and cultural forms, given how much more mystified, complicated, vast, and interconnected our societies have become in the twenty-first century. But these factors urge us all the more to the ruthless critique of all that exists in the present.

For a Ruthless Critique of All That Exists is thus intended as a manifesto of sorts, with a strong polemical strand complemented by a more positive argument about the role of criticism in the present. The emergence and prevalence of a "postcritical" paradigm can be seen in not only literary criticism—as widely popularized by Rita Felski's influential book *The*

Limits of Critique, among other recent works—but in social commentary more broadly, where a hegemonic "realism" sets the outer boundaries and inner limits on what sort of thinking is permissible. (If Felski's work comes in for harsher and more pervasive criticism in what follows, that is not so much because hers is the most egregious as it is because her work has been the most celebrated and influential, complete with glowing treatments in both the journalistic and academic press, along with lucrative grants and lofty titles.) I find this postcritical attitude is at once symptomatic and (perhaps unconsciously) supportive of a system that has naturalized the idea that it is total, complete, and insuperable. Radical alternatives are no longer to be even speculated upon, as the emphasis is placed on superficial or technical modifications that in themselves are presented as "solutions."

It is as if the "End of History"—one more like Francis Fukuyama's version from his famous 1989 article, later expanded into *The End of History and the Last Man,* than Hegel's grander vision from the nineteenth century—has come to fruition for many postcritical critics, who see little need to think beyond the merest technicalities of everyday life as it presents itself to the unreflective reader. Fukuyama had asserted, in what might be now thought of as a proleptic announcement of something like capitalist realism, that what seemed to some as merely the end of the Cold War was really "the end of history as such: that is, the end point of mankind's ideological evolution and the universalization of Western liberal democracy as the final form of human government" (11). Marxism as an ideology is thereby apparently vanquished, but so are any other forms of ideology critique, which would no longer be needed in such a post-ideological age. Advocates for postcritique would seem to fall in with this view, and their sort of "End of Theory" discourse sometimes echoes the triumphal voices of that post-Cold War moment. In what might be thought of as a ruse of history, these postmodern technocrats frequently present their case in terms of saving the humanities and making literary and cultural studies more relevant, even as so much of their arguments appear to be carrying water for a neoliberal regime bent on defunding the humanities in particular, higher education more broadly, and the very notion of the public good or commonweal. *For a Ruthless Critique of All That Exists* is in the first place intended as a critical engagement with and polemic against this multifaceted yet persistent tendency in criticism today.

However, I hope that this operates at a level beyond the polemical, for even those who cannot look into the seeds of time to see what grains will grow must nevertheless attempt to think through and act upon the question of what is to be done. As with Marx, who recognized that the future could not be predicted and that the task of those interested in changing the world involved the "ruthless criticism of all that exists," I advocate a reinvigorated, strengthened critical theory and practice suited to combat the ostensible impasse of the imagination in contemporary culture. I assert that the proper attitude of the humanities today is fundamentally critical, and that the humanities and literature in particular, as fields devoted to educating the imagination and interpreting texts, are most urgently needed to sound out the hollow idols of the present and to conjure up radical alternatives. In this manner, literary studies maintains a utopian dimension, not in the simplistic and crude sense of laying out the blueprints of some idealized system, but in the sense of "invoking hope," as Phillip E. Wegner puts it, by engaging in those creative reading practices associated with literary analysis, interpretation, and theory, which in turn form the basis for critique.

This work follows from my other books on the spatial imagination, critical theory, narrative, and utopia, but it is also somewhat more personal in that the issues discussed here are so closely connected to the reading, teaching, and writing that occupies me in my vocation as a literature professor. Although one necessarily tries to avoid *taking personally* arguments with which one disagrees (at least, so long as they are not *ad hominem* attacks on one's person), one cannot always avoid feeling affronted, particularly where friends and colleagues are concerned. I have dedicated this book to my old teacher and friend, Fredric Jameson, whose love for and respect of literature is so boundless that he has spent a lifetime insisting that literary studies, like the works of culture that are studied in that field, expand its horizons to properly encompass the range of human experience so vividly present in literature itself. Bizarrely, some scholars have tended to lament that such an approach as Jameson's "reduces" the text to the political, the ideological, the social, or whatever, whereas it is they who wish to most restrictively circumscribe and police the boundaries of literature's provenance and spheres of influence. As Jameson himself has said, "[t]he stereotypical characterization of such enlargement as *reductive* remains a never-ending source of hilarity." That those who have lobbied in favor of reparative reading, surface reading, or postcritique have often chosen Jameson and his work as their principal antagonists (or straw men) does not surprise me, but I confess, it never fails to irritate me. Hence, if Jameson's work, and Marxist criticism more generally, emerges as an exemplary approach to literature in what follows, that will come as no surprise either. But it is largely because Marxist critique offers the most inclusive and generous practice of creative reading, connected as it always is to a commitment to human imagination and to the social organizations best suited to empower it for everyone.

For a Ruthless Critique of All That Exists is divided into four chapters, plus this Introduction and a Conclusion. Chapter 1, "The Enervated Imagination," takes up the challenge of contemporary capitalist realism, the pervasive feeling that the present economic, political, and social systems cannot be fundamentally altered, although reforms here and there may be permitted. The enervated imagination, however, is not just some natural decline in speculative powers over the years, but a key component of the modern capitalist system itself, all the more powerfully instantiated with a neoliberalism that establishes a mystical "market," extended to the global scale, as the dominant if not sole motor and influence of the world in which we live. In this chapter I examine the ways in which the imaginative faculties are limited by contemporary ideological pressures before considering just how recent developments in social, cultural, and literary criticism have—in some cases, inadvertently—contributed to this phenomenon. I argue that the fashionable embrace of surface reading and postcritique, along with such trends as thin description, weak thought, ordinary language philosophy, computational criticism, distant reading, and object-oriented ontology, has served to abet the forces that would limit the imagination and impose strictures upon creative speculation, thus capitulating to the apologists of a system who would have us believe that there can be no alternatives.

In Chapter 2, "Boundless Mystification," I discuss the odd timing of the postcritical movement, which has argued against ideology critique and in favor of "just reading" (to cite Sharon Marcus's phrase) at a moment and mostly in a society that is characterized by the most forceful and pervasive levels of ideological mystification in history. In response to "the objection of the ordinary reader, when confronted with elaborate or ingenious interpretations, that the text means just what it says," Jameson in *The Political Unconscious* observes, "Unfortunately, no society has ever been quite so mystified in quite so many ways as our own, saturated as it is with messages and information, the very vehicles of mystification" (60–61). This insight lies at the core of Marxist literary criticism, in which the interpretation of texts has frequently, and assiduously, involved ideology critique. That is, the critic attempts to disclose both the ideological content or structural limitations of a given text while also being attuned to the text's utopian or revolutionary potential. In recent decades, Marxist criticism in particular and what is taken to be the hermeneutics of suspicion more generally have come under attack by literary scholars who favor various forms of postcritique, including surface reading and thin description. The timing for this seems especially bad and even "suspicious," as our own era—with the world wide web of constantly shifting information, fake news, sponsored journalistic content, social media scandals, and complex yet stark and perhaps intractable ideological divides—appears to be far more complex than even the postindustrial "society of the spectacle" to which Jameson was responding in 1981. In this chapter, I argue that postcritique, along with all that it involves, contributes to the disempowerment of the imagination and thus serves to lend support to the contemporary powers that be, advertently or otherwise. This means that postcritique, at an ideological level, necessarily also contributes to the radical dismantling of higher education caused by rampant neoliberalism. The vocation of ideology critique and of Marxist criticism is, I believe, the most appropriate response to a society so utterly mystified as our own.

Chapter 3, "Critique Unlimited," examines the ways that this postcritical approach to literature has joined with and supported a tendency toward antitheory in the humanities. Looking more closely at Felski's celebrated study *The Limits of Critique* in this context, I argue against a postcritical approach to literature that would eschew interpretation in favor of description, affect, and enjoyment. In recent years, the advocacy for a postcritical approach and the critical resistance to that approach, and thus the affirmation of the value of critique itself, have formed one of the more animated debates within literary and cultural studies in the United States and elsewhere. At the same time, perhaps ironically, critique seems more necessary and desirable than ever in confronting contemporary reality in the USA and beyond. In this chapter, I discuss current debates over postcritical approaches to literature, offer my considered objections to Felski's position and arguments, and call for a more nuanced understanding of critique, the employment of which is all the more desirable both for literary studies and for interpreting the world we live in today.

Chapter 4, "Reading Adorno by the Pool," takes its title from a memorable line in *Late Marxism*, where Jameson wondered aloud whether Theodor Adorno's famous assertion that "there can be no poetry after Auschwitz" needed to be updated in the era of a triumphal, consumerist postmodernism. As Jameson put it, "[t]he question about poetry after Auschwitz has been replaced with that of whether you could bear to read Adorno and Horkheimer next to the pool." The heady delirium of that "End of History" moment of the early 1990s had given way to greater cultural anxieties and sociopolitical conundrums, but the attacks on critical theory have become all the stronger since then. One motivation behind them is the desire to "sell" a postcritical approach to the public. For example, Felski has argued that "critique" itself has alienated literature professors from the broader public, and that the postcritical approach to literature will reconnect scholars with the public at large. Others with completely different approaches, such as Franco Moretti and his embrace of "distant reading," also argued for the need for literary studies to abandon critical reading in favor of a practice facilitated by, and suited to, the interests of Silicon Valley. As I discuss in this chapter, these sorts of theories of literature, reading, and teaching underwrite practices expressly designed for public consumption, which is part of its problem. By appealing to the mass market, they must bask in what Jameson called "the polluted sunshine of the shopping mall," averting their gaze from or perhaps blind to the various ideological commitments that their adherents have made by promoting these theories. I will argue for the ongoing need for a less commodified, more overtly critical literary theory and practice that can disclose the cleansing gloom that is opposed to this false light. Countering these mostly antitheoretical approaches, I defend "high" theory and make a case for an intensive return to theory that can help us to recognize, challenge, and ultimately move beyond the limits currently placed on the critical imagination in twenty-first-century cultural discourse.

Finally, in the Conclusion, "Recipes for the Cook-Shops of the Future," I attempt to show more positively the utopian dimension of critique. When a young Marx called for "a ruthless criticism of all that exists," he did so in recognition that "constructing the future and settling everything for all times are not our affair." Nearly 30 years later, in the Afterword to the second (German) edition of *Capital*, Marx irritably notes that a French reviewer had criticized him for "confining myself to the critical analysis of actual facts, instead of writing receipts...for the cook-shops of the future." Clearly, the desire for a glimpse into the future remains strong, even as the impossibility of achieving it is widely acknowledged. Although prophecy and predictions are not realistic, "the dialectic of utopia and ideology," as Jameson has termed it, discloses the ways in which even the most total systems of domination or control can have the potential for liberatory reversals and breakthroughs that may lay the foundations for new spaces altogether. Critical theory, alongside its committed critical practice, can make possible new ways of seeing and imagining, allowing us to detect what Ernst Bloch called that "gold-bearing rubble" amid the present disaster, and enabling a sense of hope against the all-too-commonly-held belief in the impossibility of change. In this concluding chapter, I discuss the utopian impulse at the heart of critical theory, which itself stands athwart the hegemonic capitalist realism tacitly or expressly embraced by the postcritical forces. The call for a ruthless critique of all that exists is, after all, fundamentally a phase in the process of imagining radically different worlds and lives, which has always been the vocation of creative writing and literary representation. Critique thus joins with *poiesis* in helping us to understand our world and to attempt to transform it into a world worth living in.

Foucault's definition of *critique* as the art of voluntary insubordination aptly reaffirms Marx's call for a ruthless criticism of all that exists, shrinking "neither from its own discoveries, nor from conflict with the powers that be." It is, as Marx says, an "attempt to discover the new world through the critique of the old." Literature itself is one of the ways in which the critical attitude has most effectively expressed its insubordination toward the powers that be, in various ways and with diverse effects, and literature is always discovering new worlds even as it engages with the older ones. Those who love literature, who love its power to educate and to fire the imagination, must also come down on the side of critique, which helps to make possible literature's own ability to interpret, and thus help to change, the world.

Chapter 1

The Enervated Imagination

In one of the more memorable, if somewhat perplexing, slogans from the late 1960s, radical protesters enjoined the people to "Be realistic: Demand the Impossible!"

The juxtaposition of these two phrases in a single assertion obviously represents its own form of satire. There is a clearly ludic quality to the saying, what with its paradox so blatantly stated. Having been assured throughout our lifetimes (by parents, teachers, coaches, bosses, various public and private authorities, and so forth) that "being" realistic is a virtue, that "demanding" anything is not viewed with favor, and that the "impossible" by definition is something unworthy of our desires, we must surely conclude the old slogan is merely quaint nonsense of the hippie days, more akin to feelin' groovy or to tuning in, turning on, and dropping out than to rigorous social critique or to revolutionary political movements. And yet today, in this era of capitalist realism, the expression might find new life under altered circumstances, for demanding the impossible now seems not only a desirable step in the direction of achieving common goals, but also the necessary and even realistic approach to the global challenges we face. As climate-change activist Greta Thunberg—that unexpected, unforeseen champion, patron saint, and tutelary spirit of the legacy of the oppositional intellectual of our time—has put it, "Doing our best is no longer good enough. We must now do the seemingly impossible."

The urgency of this injunction is undeniable, at least to those who have been paying attention and who are not beholden to interests whose business it is to deny the undeniable, but the paradox remains. It is difficult to imagine how to do the seemingly impossible. To cite another expression from that mist-enveloped region of the past, one made famous from the Paris militants of *May '68*, doing the impossible will first require "Power to the Imagination!" (*l'imagination au pouvoir*). Jean-Paul Sartre at the time observed in *Le Nouvel Observateur* that this slogan, and the concept embedded within it, represented "an extension of the field of the possible," while marveling at how difficult this idea had been even to think in the decades leading up to that moment. An empowered imagination, suddenly freed to think otherwise about those things that had previously been unimagined and unthought, certainly could expand the boundaries that had kept the putative field of possibility so narrow and hemmed in. Demanding the impossible appears far less Quixotic once one reimagines the world in which possibilities had been so cruelly circumscribed.

This is also the message of another great theorist of that epoch, Herbert Marcuse, who in *Eros and Civilization* extolled the utopian character of the Great Refusal, as he called it, on display among those—artists, activists, critics, and so on—who could not passively accept the "reality principle" and go on living life according to the pre-approved scripts of a "one-dimensional society," but who insisted upon trying to develop a more livable society, "a struggle for the ultimate form of freedom": "to live without anxiety (*ohne Angst leben* [Marcuse cites Theodor Adorno here])" (149–150). Elsewhere Marcuse noted that, in his time, "any transformation of the technical and natural environment is a possibility" and that "the locus of possibility is historical," thus subject to change ("The End of Utopia," 62). Hence, for Marcuse, a phrase like "Be realistic: Demand the impossible!" was not so much a semantic paradox as a social and political imperative. Andrew T. Lamas recently summed it up nicely: "'Demand the impossible!'...from a Marcusean perspective, means *demand that which the system has labeled impossible but which can be delivered through a reorganization of the society's priorities and procedures"* (107). The idea is not abstract or theoretical at all, even if it is profoundly critical. One need only hear for the zillionth time that the United States cannot afford to provide relief to victims of poverty and disease, while in the same breath being told that the multi-million-dollar-per-minute costs of bombing of this or that enemy *du jour* is not only possible, but advisable, necessary, and in any event already happening whether you like it or not...this says all one needs to hear about what is or is not "possible" among the demands of the people. And yet we hear it all the time.

My references to the 1960s, to such emblematic thinkers of that time as Sartre and Marcuse, to *les évènements de mai* and its memorable graffiti (*sous les pavés, le plage!*), or to the protests in the street and in the realm of ideas are not made out of any sense of nostalgia. As the many autopsies of that epoch have made clear, these movements had more than their share of problems, and the concatenation of their variously utopian activities and aims undoubtedly helped to make possible much of the apparently dystopian programs of the 1970s and 1980s, throughout both culture and society. Nevertheless, this momentary efflorescence of widespread and radically imaginative thinking does provide an occasion for better understanding what Mark Fisher would later characterize as "capitalist realism." The contrast could not be starker between heterogenous collectivities demanding the impossible and urging the empowerment of the imagination on the one hand, and on the other, the widespread sense only a decade or two later that not only could the socioeconomic and political organization of the present not be meaningfully altered in practice, but that such a change is also somehow *unimaginable*. In the twenty-first century, this sort of repressive "realism" places strict limits on the social imagination.

"It Is Easier to Imagine the End of the World. . ."

By now it has become a cliché, or perhaps just a truism, to say that it seems easier for most people today to imagine the end of the world than to imagine the end of capitalism. It is amusing, not to mention noteworthy, that the now famous observation circulates so easily that its origin is disputed, albeit with avuncular good cheer rather than with jealousy or bitterness. The phrase is variously attributed to Fredric Jameson, Slavoj Žižek, or even to Fisher, who himself cites both Jameson and Žižek, while averring that the slogan—"it is easier to imagine the end of the world than it is to imagine the end of capitalism"—captures the essence of "capitalism realism." As Sean Grattan has pointed out in *Hope Isn't Stupid*, "[t]hat the phrase circulates as a somehow unattributable truism says a lot about what kinds of futures might remain unthinkable after the much heralded end of history" (5).

It has been such a commonplace saying in recent years that the question of attribution has become a sort of inside joke. For instance, in a 2003 essay later included in his revised and expanded collection, *The Ideologues of Theory*, Jameson himself reiterated the claim but introduced it with the wry, indefinite "someone once said" formulation: "Someone once said that it is easier to imagine the end of the world than to imagine the end of capitalism" (573). Jameson probably does deserve the credit (or blame) for the phrase, if only because Žižek himself cites Jameson in his own version of it, but the two Marxist theorists undoubtedly enjoy seeing the conflation of sources, even if they lament the "truth" of the assertion.

Jameson's original formulation, whose slight difference might be said to make all the difference, appears in his underrated study of utopia and postmodernism, *The Seeds of Time*, where he says, "[i]t seems to be easier for us today to imagine the thoroughgoing deterioration of the earth and of nature than the breakdown of late capitalism; perhaps that is due to some weakness in our imagination" (xii). Meanwhile, Žižek's "original" version of the saying quotes Jameson in the context of discussing the persistence of ideology in the supposedly post-ideological age we now remember as the early-to-mid-1990s. As Žižek writes in "The Spectre of Ideology,"

> Up to a decade or two ago, the system of production-nature (man's productive-exploitative relationship with nature and its resources) was perceived as a constant, whereas everybody was busy imagining different forms of the social organization of production and commerce (Fascism and Communism as alternatives to liberal capitalism); today, as Fredric Jameson has perspicaciously remarked, nobody seriously considers possible alternatives to capitalism any longer, whereas popular imagination is persecuted by visions of the forthcoming "breakdown in nature," of the stoppage of all life on earth—it seems easier to imagine the "end of the world" than a far more modest change in the mode of production, as if liberal capitalism is the "real" that will somehow survive even under conditions of global ecological catastrophe. (1)

Tellingly, Jameson and Žižek both place emphasis on the power of the imagination, and I therefore think it is important to remember that, for all the catchiness of the phrases "end of the world" and "end of capitalism," the real issue raised by this now-familiar dictum is whether and how well we are capable of imagining alternatives to conditions in which we find ourselves at present.

How did we get here, to a place where not only are alternatives to capitalist modes of organizing our lives unimaginable, but this idea is so obvious as to need no definitive citation? It is like saying that the earth revolves around the sun (with all due respect to Galileo and Copernicus, of course). Needless to say, perhaps, our condition today is overdetermined, and any attempt to pin down the one primary cause will readily be understood as simplistic and inadequate. In the early aftermath of the 1980s, for example, a number of critics cited the "end of the Cold War" as evidence of there being no alternative to USA-styled capitalism, which in turn foreclosed upon even speculating about alternatives, as if somehow the images of Leonid Brezhnev, Nicolae Ceauşescu, the KGB, or the Stasi were the only ones keeping our imaginations active all those years. But even before *glasnost* and *perestroika* in the Soviet Union, the rise and spread of neoliberalism was well underway, with the transformation of the global economy in the aftermath of the Bretton Woods collapse, the oil crises and recessions of the 1970s, and the increasingly visible signs of what would later be called globalization. Neoliberal dogma, manifest in its political forms of Thatcherism and Reaganism, but quickly taken to heart by what might have been called Blairism and Clintonism in the 1990s, was fundamentally economic, but its ideological influence has been felt on all areas of social life, right down to the ways people read, write, and think about the world.

Following critics such as Jameson, I have suggested elsewhere that the paradox of the enervated imagination involves a related problem, specifically the crisis of representation implicit in any attempt to give meaningful form to the social totality in the present. The planetary scale of our social relations under a system of globalization involves us in a web of almost inconceivably complex and vast networks in which we are entangled. A reason why many suddenly find it so easy to imagine the "end of the world" and so difficult to imagine the end of our now global, socioeconomic system is because the spatio-political figures previously used to stand in for our sense of place or our frame of reference—local, regional, national, or even continental geopolitical zones—no longer function as effectively in our efforts to map the world system today.

Arguably, the burgeoning of new forms of nationalist and racist movements in different parts of the world today is a sign of the times, but also of the failure of the imagination to think beyond the older, retrograde and reactionary models. Earlier generations could think in terms of region or nation, a luxury now reserved for the most benighted and reactionary elements of many societies, whose sheer blindness to the ways of the world today can be registered in the perplexities of transnational finance alone, never mind the thoroughly imbricated matters of production, trade, energy policies, diplomatic and military relations, ecological development and degradation, and so on. There is an apocalyptic character to this thinking that finds its counterparts in a popular culture dominated by dystopian visions. One reason that the end of the world may be easier to imagine than the end of capitalism is that the former seems more realistic, partly because people feel that we are already experiencing an end-of-the-world in progress, that we are "living in the end times," as Žižek has put it. What Jürgen Habermas has referred to as the *postnational constellation* requires an alternative order of social thinking, which in turn would require different representational techniques and forms. Hence, the crucial role of the educated and empowered imagination at the very moment when various forces and circumstances conspire to constrain the imagination.

From Critical Theory to Cultural Studies

Within its admittedly small sector, but one intimately tied to all of the others through the various networks of power and money in an age of globalization, literary studies has been one of the areas affected by the forces and circumstances. Although I would not argue that there is some clear historical parallelism between the social, economic, and political transformations over the past 50 years and permutations of academic literary criticism and scholarship during that time, the latter has undoubtedly been influenced by, if not totally bound up in, the former in manifold ways, both visible and less so. To be sure, a fuller history of the institutions—for instance, Bill Readings's *The University in Ruins* and Christopher Newfield's *The Great Mistake: How We Wrecked Public Universities and How We Can Fix Them*—can illuminate these connections between educational and social policies, but part of the story also lies within the disciplinary fields of the literary humanities themselves. Such an internal history would in no way discount the bigger picture, but it can show how what might seem the very parochial concerns of a tiny number of intellectuals may contribute to the larger processes of neoliberal ideology and capitalist realism.

A version of that story would perhaps include the narrative of "the rise and fall of theory," which frequently gets positioned as its own post-1960s adventure in which the revolutionaries of that era emerge and thrive only to then die off, become domesticated, recant their votes, or some other manner of decline. This trajectory fits well into those related narratives of hippies becoming yuppies or the academic equivalent, "tenured radicals" (even though the popularizer of that term, Roger Kimball, unironically viewed such tweedy former revolutionaries as true threats to truth, justice, and the American way). In the case of French theory in particular, whose intellectual and transatlantic voyages are entertainingly discussed by François Cusset, the phantom of May '68 looms large, even if most of the great "theory" generation emerging from that decade and then coming to prominence in the USA in the 1970s was not directly part of those *événements*. Famously, Michel Foucault wasn't even in France at the time, and the militant students and workers were hardly likely to chant lines from *Le mots et los choses* in their protests. Jacques Derrida's revolutionary activities at the time were largely confined to the page, and Jameson has quipped that, lacking its own versions of the bacchanals of Haight-Ashbury or Greenwich Village, France was able to produce *Anti-Oedipus* instead. (In any case, the calumnies of Luc Ferry and Alain Renaut in their book, *La Pensée*

68 [translated into English with the less polemical title, *French Philosophy of the Sixties*], required to turn thinkers like Foucault and Derrida into inspirations for the uprising, were way off the mark, even if those thinkers became significant, "radical" figures for literary and cultural studies in the decades that followed). The introduction of structuralist and poststructuralist theory, combined with and sometimes contributing to new forms of Marxist, psychoanalytic, and feminist theory, which in turn had been aided by recent translations into English of key earlier works, made for a heady mixture of new and transformative ideas for the study and appreciation of literature.

If literature is already a great font and inspiration for the human imagination, then the rise of "Theory-with-a-capital-T" had the effect of compounding that power exponentially, at least in some quarters. Linguistic and stylistic theories helped to inform the way texts were not only interpreted, offering new meanings, but also how they were understood in their own being, such that what constituted a literary text itself was a matter for fitful contemplation and raucous debate. Critics drawing upon the traditions of thought emanating from those "masters of suspicion" (as Paul Ricoeur called them), Marx, Nietzsche, and Freud, helped to disclose crucial aspects of a given literary work's or author's social, political, or libidinal content and ramifications, even if—or especially if—such content was unconscious and such ramifications were unintended. Feminist critics uncovered aspects of patriarchy, sexual subjugation, and gender inequity in the very language used to represent the world, and also did much to reevaluate and expand the canon of literary works deemed worthy of consideration in classrooms and elsewhere. Scholars attuned to race as a social construct and historical fact demonstrated the degree to which bigotry and inequality had been both institutionalized and "naturalized" in the formation of disciplinary fields and in the teaching of literature. The "canon wars" in US higher education were themselves influenced mightily by literary and critical theory, as well as by those in social movements who argued for greater representation and inclusiveness in curricular decisions. And so on, as Kurt Vonnegut would say.

Needless to say, maybe, that all of these developments and more were met with a great deal of resistance, particularly from antitheory scholars within the various institutions of literature (i.e., university faculties, but also journals, conferences, etc.) and skeptics from outside academe (especially in the form of Op-Ed pieces and politically motivated pronouncements bemoaning the attacks on Western Civilization and the Great Books). There was also plenty of debate within the precincts of literary theory whose sound and fury undoubtedly caught the attention of those on the other side of the fence, who then formed opinions based on hearsay. As I discuss in chapters 3 and 4, the resistance to theory was already strong even during theory's putative heyday, and although its effects have been widespread and transformative, it is probably safe to say that theory never dominated academic literary studies in the United States, even if some of its key figures did become "stars" of a sort. Critical theory, in supplementing the power of literature to fire and to educate the imagination, was and remains a crucial part of the literary humanities. By the turn of the new century, however, even such wildly influential proponents as Terry Eagleton—whose bestselling *Literary Theory: An Introduction* quite literally introduced hundreds of thousands of students to the topic—could publish a book with the title *After Theory* and thus concede that an epochal shift had occurred in the field.

Eagleton is an odd one to complain, since his own *Literary Theory* and later work on the ideology of the aesthetic had called for an end to "literature" itself, but in *After Theory* he identifies two critical tendencies that have displaced, if not replaced, "theory" in contemporary literary studies: *sex*, by which he seems to indicate the vast expansion of sexuality studies in general, but which he parodies as a more lurid interest in titillating topics, and *culture*, by which he means a sort of intemperate obsession with products of popular culture rather than the critical legacies of Raymond Williams or Walter Benjamin. He does note that one of the great achievements of cultural theory had been to place these subjects on the critical map, only to see the epigones of a later generation water down their import even as they celebrated the subjects. One cannot help but detect a bit of that stereotypical old-guy crabbiness ("You kids, get off my lawn!") in Eagleton's assessment, but he manages in his own manner to get at the ways in which theory had become somewhat domesticated by the 1990s, notwithstanding the significant work also being done in literary and cultural criticism at the time. Yet Eagleton also identifies a tendency that more closely connects his concerns to my own in this book; that is, the ways in which these critical tendencies abandoned, replaced, and attacked Marxist theory in particular. Related to this is a general tendency toward abandoning critique in favor of other modes of discussion, which in turn has contributed to a sort of circumscribing of possibilities for imagining alternatives. Brilliant though much of this work has been, it too has contributed to the enervation of the imagination in the literary humanities.

Substitutes for Marxism

Given the innately political character of sexuality and cultural studies, it may seem odd to suspect that these approaches depoliticized theory and the humanities. Most of the work done in gender and sexuality studies, like cultural studies, is overtly political, and much of it comes in the form of oppositional criticism. Emerging from the real-world battles of the Women's and Civil Rights movements, as well as from mass culture, politics, and history, these areas of inquiry have always been animated by a spirit of protest, but have in effect come to be part of the rejection of Marxism, even if many of the scholars involved were formed in part or whole within a Marxist tradition.

In a lengthy review essay on cultural studies (specifically, on the huge collection of essays called *Cultural Studies* edited by Lawrence Grossberg, Cary Nelson, and Paula A. Treichler, which was itself the product of a major conference held at the University of Illinois, Champaign-Urbana in 1990) included in *The Ideologies of Theory,* Jameson assessed the degree to which "Cultural Studies" had already become a "substitute" for Marxism, notwithstanding its august prehistory in the cultural materialism of Raymond Williams and other fellow travelers whose militant interventions had almost always been motivated by socialist politics. Indeed, the foundational "schools" of cultural studies were arguably Marxist from the outset. I would say that academic cultural studies can trace its roots to at least three distinctive theoretical or critical traditions, each of which draws heavily from Marxist theory of one type or another: (1) A primarily British school, associated especially with the Birmingham School and names like Williams and Stuart Hall, which developed from the sort of working-class histories of Richard Hoggart, E. P. Thompson, and Christopher Hill, and thus maintained strong ties to Marxist theory and socialist politics (in the work of Eric Hobsbawm, for instance); (2) A German variant, labeled the Frankfurt School, with its foundations in both Marxist theory and the sociological work of Max Weber, Georg Simmel, and others, plus considerations of Freudian psychology in looking at "mass culture"; and (3) a more semiotics-oriented approach, perhaps best exemplified in Roland Barthes's *Mythologies* and such subsequent studies as *The Fashion System, Camera Lucida,* or *Empire of Signs,* along with dozens of essays in which elements from *la vie quotidienne* were subjected to a structuralist version of ideology critique (one might also mention Henri Lefebvre's work as well, and

Debord's *The Society of the Spectacle*). As distinctive, and at times opposed, as these "schools" and their methods were to one another, they all drew force from a close connection to Marxism, which itself has been variously understood at different times and by different theorists. As Jameson notes, it is partly the postmodernist (i.e., from Jean-François Lyotard's understanding of it in *The Postmodern Condition*) rejection of *grand récits*—that is, "that Cultural Studies does not do Grand Theory anymore" (610)—that leads newer practitioners of cultural studies to abandon Marxism, but there is also a distinct change in political perspective in which the fragmented or isolated "politics of unmixed identity" takes precedence over the presumptive solidarities and mélange of class.

Along these lines, one might mention other practices and trends that have contributed heavily to the rise and prominence of cultural studies. Most notably, the great expansion in the range of texts to be considered that came with film studies, media studies, and so forth, not to mention the pressures from the "new social movements" (as they were then called) help shape both the approaches to artifacts of culture and the selection of artifacts under critical consideration (e.g., pulp fiction, popular music, and so on). However, at their core, these types of cultural studies often had participated in the Marxist tradition by calling attention to the *ideological* nature of these texts and their function in modern societies, which in turn meant focusing on the imaginary relationships to the real-world situations. Those critics still believed in the power of the imagination and, as a character in Kim Stanley Robinson's *Red Mars* put it, "they [i.e., Marxists] acknowledged that the imagination was a powerful force in human life" (460). Critique, including ideology critique, maintained its pride of place among the various critical activities associated with cultural studies.

But as practitioners moved away from Marxism *per se*, whether opting for a sort of *post-Marxist* position (à la Ernesto

Laclau and Chantal Mouffe's *Hegemony and Socialist Strategy*), abandoning the tradition entirely in favor of non-Marxist or even anti-Marxist perspectives, or even adopting a somewhat hybrid form that, say, included the insights of Gramsci's or Williams's cultural criticism while jettisoning the Marxist theory and socialist politics that undergirded it, the emphasis on critique itself also diminished. Arguably, the cultural studies of the new millennium would entail, not so much the interpretation and evaluation of texts, as the staging of various contests among competing interests at the level of straightforward content, registering or adjudicating a given author's or text's position vis-à-vis others' based on something like surface reading, inasmuch as merely describing the phenomena (itself a form of interpretation, of course, since any description of something entails a sense of metacommentary) could replace the search for "hidden" or latent meanings. The political was increasingly performative, and the performance, not its underlying conditions or potential effects, was what mattered.

Perhaps most influential during this period in which critical theory, Marxist critique in particular, was waning is the emergence and burgeoning hegemony of postcolonial discourses, some of whose origins also lay among the Marxist critiques of imperialism and in Marxian world systems theory, among other critical territories. Decades before Edward W. Said's *Orientalism*, which nevertheless is often cited as the postcolonial studies' field-establishing work, Marxist critics (among others) had laid the foundation for postcolonial theory in the rigorous critique of imperialism in connection with the critique of capitalism and its ideologies. Said's work, along with that of Homi Bhabha, Gayatri Chakravorty Spivak, and Aijaz Ahmad, to name only a few superstars from the field in the 1990s, has inspired an extraordinary body of critical research, not only into the specific relations among colonizing powers and colonial subjects, but also into the ways that empire and its ramifications worldwide affect cultural production on nearly every level. Postcolonial theory has, in turn, breathed new life into areas not always focused on such imperial connections, including American literature or medieval studies. However, as postcolonial studies has become more wide-ranging and influential, it too seems to have become an alternative to Marxism inasmuch as his political perspective shifts attention away from the material conditions of the possibility and spread of empire, in favor of an almost transcendental sense of the relations between a metropolitan center and an "Other," which can then be conveniently transferred into other situations with vastly different historical conditions.

This is, in part, Ahmad's as well as Vivek Chibber's critique of Said's vision of Orientalism, which becomes the source of colonial exploitation rather than an ideological justification of the capitalist extension into new territories. By reversing the polarity of ideology and material conditions, such a perspective can tend to reify race, ethnicity, culture, nationality, or other such frameworks for identity in order to then ignore the real motivations and factors leading to the colonization of disparate lands and control over their inhabitants. For it is *culture*, far more than political economy (never mind class struggle or mode of production), that then explains the colonial system and its enduring aftermath. As Chibber says of Said's foundational concept,

> colonialism now appears not as the consequence of developments particular to a certain era, but as an expression of a deeper ontological divide between East and West, a symptom of the cultural orientation of Europe's inhabitants. We have gone from the culprit being British capitalists to its being "the West"—from classes to cultures.

In so doing, postcolonial studies becomes intertwined with

cultural studies, just as it sidesteps or opposes Marxism, and given the innately political context in which its rhetoric operates, it cannot but be attractive as a form of oppositional criticism even as it tends to remove the critic from the actual fray.

The evolution of postcolonial studies into something far less interested in ideology as the justification of material interests and more of a commentary on relations among relatively stable identities corresponds with the rise of the newer forms of cultural studies and, perhaps also, with the predominance of work focused on sexuality. Again, much of this work was extremely valuable and even necessary, placing crucial but formerly overlooked matters back into the discussion. In so doing, they made up for some unforgivable omissions or marginalizations, as well as correcting a number of fundamental errors, in literary studies. The beneficial results of cultural studies, postcolonial theory, and sexuality studies are enormous, and ought not to be downplayed. However, in the wake of their successes, these fields of criticism have also contributed, perhaps inadvertently and probably unintentionally, to the assault on theory and on critique that has become so prominent in recent decades.

Paranoia and Postcritique

Although precursors could be identified, the turning point in the turn away from critical theory and the practice of critique in literary studies is often located at the publication of Eve Kosofsky Sedgwick's influential essay "Paranoid Reading and Reparative Reading, or, You're So Paranoid, You Probably Think This Essay Is about You," which first appeared (in a slightly different form) in 1997 as the editorial introduction to a collection of essays *Navel Gazing: Queer Readings in Fiction*, but is probably best known now as a chapter in her book *Touching Feeling: Affect, Pedagogy, Performance* (2003). In *The Limits of Critique*, Rita Felski cites it first above all in listing works by "a growing groundswell of voices" to which hers is joined in attacking the "ethos" of critique. That Sedgwick should be an originary presence for the surface readers and postcritical critics may seem odd, given her stature as significant feminist critic and a founding figure within queer theory, discourses that have been known to investigate beyond mere appearances and to criticize latent or hidden power relations. Nevertheless, Sedgwick's essay on "paranoid reading," and by extension Sedgwick herself, has become essential touchstone and authority for the postcritical paradigm in contemporary literary studies.

In establishing this dyadic opposition and in popularizing the view that literary interpretation is motivated by a sort of paranoia, Sedgwick's essay arguably did damage to both literary studies as a whole and to queer theory in particular. Such is the view of David Kurnick, who observes in "A Few Lies: Queer Theory and Our Method Melodramas" that Sedgwick's essay served to install a "sclerotic" binary "at the heart of our so-called method debates"; in addition, Kurnick says,

> it authorized that binary as a covert characterology; it encouraged a confusion about the difference between mood and method, and the relations between them (differences and relations of which Sedgwick herself is elsewhere a superlative analyst), and to that extent instantiated a turn away from questions of literary interpretation in favor of questions of spiritual or psychological bearing. (362)

(Kurnick adds that "it positioned queer theory firmly on the wrong side of its polarized view of literary study, effectively inaugurating the amnesia about that field" to which his overall argument draws attention, which is beyond the scope of my argument.) In any event, the Sedgwick-inspired attack on "paranoid" reading, far more than the embrace of some form of "reparative" reading in fact, has proven to be the lasting legacy of this essay.

Sedgwick, whose playfulness is apparent in the title (alluding to Carly Simon's hit song from the 1970s, for example, but also passive-aggressively attacking the reader), mischievously cites Jameson's famous opening words of the Preface to *The Political Unconscious*, "Always historicize," only to then churlishly complain that the word *always* is "atemporal," asking "what could have less to do with historicizing" than that? As if Jameson himself is somehow unaware of the paradox, even though in the very next sentence (which Sedgwick and her admirers somehow always fail to quote) he affirms that the "slogan" is a "transhistorical" imperative. A brilliant and careful reader like Sedgwick knows better, but it cannot be accidental that she would choose a work of Marxist criticism in particular to lampoon. As I discuss in Chapter 2, the advocates for postcritical reading have always used Jameson in particular and Marxism more generally in their straw-men arguments, which is further evidence of their antipathy for a social and political *Weltanschauung* as much as for some critical tone, attitude, or mien. Moreover, as Kurnick had pointed out, Sedgwick's sclerotic binary had conflated "an attitude or psychic state" (paranoia) and a "project" (reparation), such that merely seeming to be a more reparative-minded person, without actually doing anything like a reparative work, is all it takes to distinguish oneself from the "cruel," "contemptuous," and "ugly" paranoid reader. Kurnick notes that no example of a reparative reading, nor any sense that it would differ in substance from a paranoid one, is ever given (365); he finds this all the more significant given that the "text" used in Sedgwick's opening example was not a poem or novel, but an informal narrative of the origins of the HIV virus. This model replaces action, even the relatively modest action of reading, with a sort of personal posturing.

In many respects, this posturing might be connected to a larger societal problem, one that is perhaps related to a neoliberal ideology that would establish the individual subject (or consumer) as the chief if not sole agent, and the moment of selection and transaction as the main event. That is, if in this circumstance—quite different from those under which the phrase was coined by feminist militants of an earlier moment—the personal is the political, then one's attitude toward a text, just like one's consumer habits, is as valuable as any analysis of it could be. The individual subject's self-fashioned identity alone confers the desired authority upon which any reading would rest, and the performance of appreciation, attachment, or affect effectively replaces the overlapping activities analysis, evaluation, and interpretation (a.k.a. critique) that would seek to make visible the text's larger and more generalized effects.

The consumerist ethos is thus given cover and elevated by discourse that is at once remarkably elite, given the status of its proponents, and rhetorically demotic, as these proponents like to situate themselves on the side of the "ordinary reader," who is somehow being praised by being considered uncritical. (So-called "lay" readers are often quite critical indeed, as many authors can confirm from experience with online forums, book signings, and so forth.) In the years since Sedgwick's influential essay appeared, a large number of prominent literary critics—many of whom occupy prestigious positions in some of the most elite universities in the United States, not to mention being affiliated with "leading" academic journals and publishing with selective, "top tier" presses—have embraced a postcritical approach, ostensibly denying the value of expertise and training which are themselves prerequisites for the positions they themselves hold. Moreover, they have done so largely by attacking other critics, especially Marxists (although these are sometimes unnamed and unidentifiable), whose commitment to critique is then cast as itself elitist or objectionably parochial. The populist rhetoric can be quite compelling, especially if the postcritical position is already flattering the readers, who are mostly other academics, of course, for their perspicacity in declining to ask questions, refusing to look beyond surfaces, and accepting the *status quo* as is and always. Somehow, that becomes not only a sign of good reading, but of good citizenship or perhaps even goodness *tout court*.

For example, Felski would like to claim that "the hermeneutics of suspicion" and the ethos surrounding "critique" are responsible for such assaults on common sense as climate-change denial (see *Hooked* 21). But a moment's reflection undermines that baseless accusation. Not only are most notorious climate-change deniers *not* typically enthusiastic readers of Marx, Nietzsche, and Freud, but many are in fact deeply committed to what might be called "surface reading." This is why commentators across all right-wing media tend to point to the thermometer on the first cold day of each autumn as "evidence" that global warming is either a liberal hoax or a simply false hypothesis. The rare "cool summer day" becomes more real-world evidence that egghead scientists, like those literary critics who somehow find unexpected or innovative significance in texts that are apparently already "just say what they mean," are full of shit. It is not that these climate skeptics view expertise with suspicion (although some undoubtedly do), so much as they celebrate the obvious truth of their own surface readings. Their "attachments" to these narratives—that is, narratives-that-will-broach-no-critique—display precisely the sort of affective power that Felski wishes to celebrate in *Hooked*, and the libidinal cathexis such skeptics maintain toward their preferred "readings" prove themselves to be quite the opposite of the pleasure of critique. If anything, the scientific community, in its insistence on delving deeper and not capitulating to merely superficial appearances, models a more thoroughly suspicious form of thinking than most hermeneutically minded critical approaches to literature would.

If the recent work of Felski comes in for an outsized share of criticism in this book, it is largely because I find it so emblematic of the problem. In what is now to be thought of as her "postcritical trilogy"—*Uses of Literature* (2008), *The Limits of Critique* (2015), and *Hooked: Art and Attachment* (2020)—Felski not only criticizes the scholarly tone and attitude that she associates with "critique," but she appears to go so far as to call for the abolition of critique and to celebrate a world in which critique would no longer be practiced (notwithstanding her own notably strong background in feminist and Frankfurt School critical theory.) That she frequently does this through the worst sorts of straw-man argumentation, essentially performing *ad hominem* attacks but without naming any *homines* in particular, is probably fitting, since it comports well with an approach that refuses to engage with particularities or to move beyond superficial appearances. It thereby contributes to the stifling of the imaginative function, even as it displays rather inventive forms of demeaning the work of her fellow literary critics.

Along those lines, the embrace of the surface level of reading and of the pleasures associated with it does not make Felski more sanguine when it comes to criticizing others. As Sheila Liming has noted in her review of *Hooked,*

> if one pauses to assess...Felski's rhetoric, what emerges is an inventory of abuse. Some of that abuse is the work of Felski's unnamed foes; but a lot of it is hers. Felski's brand of criticism "cuts aslant," "slices across," "severs," "stabs," "pulverizes," and "pries apart." The phrase "cuts across" appears with greater frequency, even, than "scission" in Hooked, suggesting that Felski may be as interested in the idea of attachment as she is in the prospect of dismemberment. This, perhaps, is what she means by "doing"—doing damage, wreaking havoc. It's a project that makes a lot of sense if one refuses the work of making sense, of explaining and accounting and engaging. For while Felski refuses to close read in this book, substituting musings on themes of

> attachment for textual analysis, she also refuses to turn and face her opponents squarely. She cites very few of them, in fact, which hampers her efforts to "cut across" and forces her, instead, to lob grenades from afar. ("Fighting Words")

Those grenades are not only lobbed from afar, but from a position of great privilege as well. Another reason why I believe Felski's postcritical program is worth devoting so much space to is that hers is arguably the most successful and celebrated. Particularly *The Limits of Critique*, which was the subject of largely appreciative forums in *PMLA*, *Religion and Literature*, and the *American Book Review*, Felski's work has received far more critical attention than many others' who are associated with these different, and maybe related, trends in literary studies. Felski has received a multimillion-dollar grant, a sum virtually unheard of for research in the humanities, to study "the uses of literature," and she has been awarded a Niels Bohr Professorship by the Danish National Research Foundation as part of this honor. Clearly, by these signs, her position is far more elevated than most academic literary critics, even among those who present themselves as radical rethinkers of their chosen fields. (It is worth noting that, prior to her celebrity as a maven of postcritique, Felski had enjoyed a deservedly excellent reputation as a feminist critic and scholar, and she remains a superb teacher, scholar, and colleague.) Not coincidentally, these honors and awards have been bestowed *for* her work on and in advancement of the postcritical approach to literature.

My thesis in this book is that the postcritical tendency in literary criticism is part, if only a relatively small part, of the crisis of the imagination that both typifies and reinforces capitalist realism today. This is not only politically debilitating, inasmuch as it tacitly enjoins us to accept and indeed celebrate the *status quo*, no matter how uncomfortable and unjust we find that status to be. It is also intellectually stultifying, as it serves to constrain our imaginative abilities and to make us accept those limits as natural, or even as desirable. I find it troubling that so many today struggle to imagine radical alternatives, but more disturbing still is the sense that literature, as a field of study, would be contributing to the enervation of the human imagination. Critique, in all its forms, appears to me all the more necessary, in literary studies and in the world around us.

Chapter 2

Boundless Mystification

In a memorable paragraph from *The Political Unconscious*, Fredric Jameson observes that interpretation "always presupposes, if not a conception of the unconscious itself, then at least some mechanism of mystification or repression in terms of which it would make sense to seek a latent meaning behind a manifest one" (60). This rather straightforward acknowledgment alone marks Jameson as being in league with those whom Paul Ricoeur, in his *Freud and Philosophy*, had dubbed the "masters of suspicion" (30)—that is, Marx, Nietzsche, and Freud—who purportedly embrace if not also figuratively embody what has become known as a hermeneutics of suspicion.

Jameson goes on to recognize "the objection of the ordinary reader, when confronted with elaborate or ingenious interpretations, that the text means just what it says," but he adds the following:

> Unfortunately, no society has ever been quite so mystified in quite so many ways as our own, saturated as it is with messages and information, the very vehicles of mystification (language, as Talleyrand put it, having been given us in order to conceal our thoughts). If everything were transparent, then no ideology would be possible, and no domination either: evidently that is not the case. But above and beyond the sheer fact of mystification, we must point to the supplementary problem involved with the study of cultural or literary texts, or in other words, of narratives: for even if discursive language were to be taken literally, there is always, and constitutively, a problem about the "meaning" of narratives as such; and the problem about the assessment

> and subsequent formulation of the "meaning" of this or that narrative is the hermeneutic question. (60-61)

For Jameson, the very fact that narratives are meaningful requires an interpretive framework or hermeneutic by which one can disclose, construct, or construe that meaning, which cannot simply be "read off" the surface of the text, for even a literal interpretation is still an interpretation. What is more, given the manifold, diverse, and powerful forces of mystification in our society, interpretation is all the more necessary to get some sense of the realities obscured by them. In this view, Jameson's sense of narrative as a socially symbolic act is directly connected to a project of ideology critique.

In recent years, this sort of approach to narrative and to social criticism has come under increasing fire, as advocates of various types of "postcritical" criticism militate against approaches to literary or cultural studies that involve what they consider to be examples of the hermeneutics of suspicion, itself viewed as somehow objectionable. Rita Felski's celebrated broadside, *The Limits of Critique,* effectively holds Jameson personally responsible for establishing the culture of critique in contemporary literary studies. For instance, she asserts that "[t]he coining of the phrase 'political unconscious' was a stroke of genius that launched a thousand research projects; it captures both the overwhelming force and the essential elusiveness of the cause to which works of art are ultimately tethered" (57). Felski blames Jameson and his followers for being insufficiently "respectful, even reverential, in tone" (57), among other things, and argues for a postcritical form of reading that focuses less on interpretation and more on description; more specifically, this approach to literary studies would focus less on demystification, and more on affirmation, passion, and inspiration (187).

Felski's opposition to "critique" and call for a postcritical approach to literature joins a long and growing line of polemical proposals by critics who aim to combat the hermeneutics of suspicion in literary studies. Although I would not want to conflate them, as each has its own distinctive characteristics, Felski herself declares that she joins "a growing groundswell of voices" contributing to a postcritical "ethos" (*Limits* 8), and in a footnote she duly names Eve Kosofsky Sedgwick's discussion of paranoid versus reparative reading, Toril Moi's recent embrace of ordinary language philosophy, Stephen Best and Sharon Marcus's call for "surface reading," as well as Marcus's later development of the practice of "just reading," not to mention Graham Harman's vision of an object-oriented ontology, and most importantly Bruno Latour's insistence that critique has "run out of steam" (195–196). In a 2015 article in *The Chronicle of Higher Education*, Jeffrey J. Williams referred to such approaches as examples of "the new modesty in literary criticism," explaining that, in what seemed to be a burgeoning trend, "[l]iterary critics have become more subdued, adopting methods with less grand speculation, more empirical study, and more use of statistics or other data. They aim to read, describe, and mine data rather than make 'interventions' of world-historical importance" ("New Modesty"). However, there is nothing modest in the stridency with which these critics oppose what Best and Marcus call "symptomatic reading" and what Felski calls "critique." Indeed, their hubris in taking on what they imagine to be a dominant, widespread, and well-nigh unassailable culture of critique in academic literary studies is remarkable in its own right.

Superficial Readings

As becomes clear almost immediately to anyone reading these critics carefully, the objection to the hermeneutics of suspicion in literary studies is part of a larger attack on critical theory, and while various types of antitheory have circulated for as long as theory itself has, this particular movement seems to feature a weirdly generational backlash. Best and Marcus embrace this sense of a generational divide directly in their "Surface Reading: An Introduction," when they assert "now we do things a bit differently than they did back then" (2). The "we" of their statement undoubtably refers to not only the authors themselves, but to a larger imagined collectivity of the literary critics who are roughly the same age. The authors make clear to whom the "they" refers as well, since Jameson is specifically named as the representative of that older, and by implication less valid, form of reading. (For the record, Jameson was born in 1934, and Best and Marcus each in the mid-1960s.) Undoubtedly part of the energy and enthusiasm animating the postcritical turn involves this sense of revolutionary, not to say Oedipal, overturning of the old guard by the new. If this is the case, then a historical reading of the phenomenon might reveal the extent to which ideological processes have become all the more powerful, refined, and complex in our era than in the one in which those older, suspicious minds were formed. After all, one of the features that these variously termed postcritical approaches share is a sense that ideological mystification is no longer something to be worried about, which may be a sure sign that ideology is operating in full force.

Indeed, it is not surprising that both "surface readers" Best and Marcus and advocates of "postcritique" would choose Jameson as their principal target, for it rapidly becomes clear that Marxism is the fundamental enemy, above if also alongside Nietzschean and Freudian critical practices. The proponents of these postcritical approaches oppose the idea of ideology critique, and this opposition is, in turn, a thinly veiled—or, perhaps, not so thinly veiled—attack on Marxism. In the United States, at least, there was far more "symptomatic reading" coming from non-Marxist perspectives, such as psychoanalytic criticism, as well as feminist criticism and critical race studies, to name a few. And yet, it is certainly no accident that Jameson, widely recognized as America's leading Marxist literary critic from at least the early 1980s on, is the primary target of the postcritical criticisms, and that *The Political Unconscious* is set up as the *fons et origo* of contemporary "symptomatic reading." As Carolyn Lesjak points out in "Reading Dialectically," the public events at which "surface reading" was introduced prior to publication included a 2006 seminar of the American Comparative Literature Association, "Symptomatic Reading and Its Discontents," on the occasion of the twenty-fifth anniversary of *The Political Unconscious*, and "The Way We Read Now: Symptomatic Reading and Its Aftermaths" conference in New York in 2008, at which Jameson himself was the keynote speaker; in retrospect, Jameson's invitation to participate in that event can only be viewed as a meticulously organized trap (269, note 63). Twenty-five years after apparently laying the foundations for what was now considered the wrong way of reading, Jameson and *The Political Unconscious* were set up as the chief enemies of contemporary critical practice, and Jamesonian ideology critique—never mind its dialectical insistence on always finding the good alongside the bad in any given text—was held up as that which ails literary studies in the twenty-first century. Bruce Robbins has observed in "Not So Well Attached" that the rhetorical effect of the phrase "the way we read *now*" already situates the "surface reading" partisans on the side of what must in advance be understood as right and good, for, like the phrase in Bruno Latour's title (i.e., "Has Critique Run Out of Steam?"), "it assumes that which it would seem obliged to establish. And what it assumes, more precisely, is that history has confirmed the author's argument" (373). Ideology critique, like the Marxist theory and criticism behind it, is utterly passé from this perspective.

As if to underscore that very point, Best and Marcus quote Jameson's comment about ideology and domination, the same lines which I quoted at the beginning of this chapter, and then assert that, because images like those of the abuses at Abu Ghirab, of the aftermath of Hurricane Katrina, or of President George W. Bush's "Mission Accomplished" media event are readily available on the internet or television for all to see, interpretation is no longer necessary, for the political domination and state-sponsored falsehoods are visible on the surface of everything. Even at the time, their choice of examples seemed bizarre, and now it seems almost mad. As if those very images were not used for ideological ends! As if everyone "read" their meaning off their surfaces in exactly the same way! The naïveté of such a statement in 2009 was shocking, to be sure, but by now it must be unforgivable, given the subsequent years of Trumpism and the widespread influence of conspiracy theories in even mainstream political discourse, not to mention "fake news" and related sorts of mystifying media and content. In our time, one might say, this sort of commitment to surface readings seems to be not only a symptom of, but an overt and enthusiastic *apologia* for, what Mark Fisher termed "capitalist realism."

The irony is that this particular variety of antitheoretical and postcritical criticism should become so pervasive and popular just when it did. Is it not striking that an influential movement within the humanities should suddenly find that critique is no longer needed just as an increasingly widespread neoliberal ideology infecting virtually all sectors of social life in the United States, as elsewhere, promotes the "natural" condition of a world system characterized at once by impersonal market forces and individual freedom of choice, amid a major expansion of US military and economic aggression no less? The same neoliberal ideology features prominently in the overdetermined "crisis of higher education," of which as university professors these critics are also undoubtedly aware, that has recharacterized students as consumers and universities as providers of services and credentials, all the while obscuring the role of the financial services industry, among others, in transforming education into a mere commodity. (For instance, in the USA, the ideologically named Bankruptcy Abuse Prevention and Consumer Protection Act of 2005 [a.k.a. "the New Bankruptcy Law"], which amounted to a declaration of war on the poor, established that student loans along with most credit card debt could no longer be as easily discharged in bankruptcy—itself an action that few individuals, apart from the very rich, would ever desire to take—and thus giving the financial services industry *carte blanche* to engage in predatory lending without adverse consequences, while telling students that college education was a good "investment"; meanwhile, public funding of higher education continued its rapid decline, as befits a system in which education itself was now viewed as simply a private good for individual investors.) Bizarrely, but perhaps unsurprisingly, the proponents of postcritique justify their position precisely in terms of this neoliberal orthodoxy, proclaiming the need to "sell" literature to students who are putatively disaffected by literary criticism and who are thus currently in the market for more entertaining options. If the product were only to be marketed correctly, they seem to think, then the humanities will be saved from the infernal machinations of neoliberal capitalism, which is the very foundation of the system that would require and reward such marketing. Talk about ideology!

For readers like Felski, Best, and Marcus, among others, ideology critique is not only old fashioned, it seems, but objectionable in its very worldview, operating as it does through a hermeneutics of suspicion that seeks ever to uncover hidden, sometimes intentionally hidden, meanings. From their perspective, it is "paranoid"—a term used to better effect by Sedgwick, and applied by Best and Marcus to Jameson—to believe that there are meanings other than the most obviously visible. In the age of Bush and Cheney (and Trump too?), all domination is so obvious that it is a waste of time to interpret it. Or even to oppose it, apparently. In such a world, the surface reader's conviction that this is all there is to see far too quickly becomes the beat cop's dismissive "Nothing to see here, folks!" The phrase practically cries out for our need to inspect further and more critically. As such, it seems like awfully bad timing to abandon critique. If Jameson in 1981 was thinking of Guy Debord's "society of the spectacle," of consumer culture, multinational capitalism, and of postmodernity more generally, then how much more suspicious ought we to be in our time of the internet's world wide web of fake news, sponsored journalistic content, social media scandals, bewildering conspiracy theories, and complex yet stark ideological divides?

It is perhaps a sign of how thoroughly the hermeneutics of suspicion has pervaded my spirit that I become instantly skeptical when told that things are "just" so. Much as we may disdain the *unnecessarily complicated*, the *overly simplified* seems far more dangerous. Even more than the deliberate attempts to mislead with not-always-attributed sponsored content in our news sources, compromised journalistic ethics, and bald-face lies that now seem to permeate public discourse today, the honest belief, held by many, that there is little beyond the ordinary appearance of things is altogether pernicious. If anything, the boundless mystifications of our era call for *more hermeneutics* and *more suspicion*. Appeals to the plain, the simple, and the ordinary cannot help but serve the forces of mystification and hence, the *status quo*, if only as an unintended consequence. I agree with Phillip E. Wegner that "theory represents a call to read more widely and expansively" (9), in which case these more antitheoretical approaches prove themselves to be not only anti-interpretation, but anti-reading, inasmuch as they seek to limit in advance the possible meanings to be produced. This, too, amounts to a program that would circumscribe and constrain the power of the imagination.

"Neoliberalism Depoliticizes"

A number of other critics have pointed out how the rise of these sort of postcritical approaches has coincided, perhaps not just coincidentally, with the predominance of neoliberalism in the United States and elsewhere. To be sure, statements like Best and Marcus's denying the existence of ideology do sound far more like extensions of the political dogmas of Thatcherism and Reaganism—Thatcher's infamous pronouncement "there is no such thing as society" readily comes to mind—than they do new forms of scholarly engagement. Understandably, the proponents of surface reading, just reading, thin description, postcritique, and so on are wary of being labeled quietist, apolitical, or conservative, but that is in large part because their arguments, *on their surface*, so clearly support either the *status quo* of the neoliberal state or the *status quo ante* of some more reactionary formation, such as the call for the return to ethics or aesthetics or mere affective enjoyment, in one form or another. And as Paul A. Bové has noted, referring in particular to Felski's *Uses of Literature*, "Felski proselytizes for the individuating processes of neoliberal consumption and narcissism, definitive forms of the contemporary 'real'" (*Love's Shadow* 407).

Felski asserts that "questioning critique is not a shrug of defeat or a hapless capitulation to conservative forces," but that "it is motivated by a desire to articulate a positive vision for humanistic thought in the face of growing skepticism about its value" (186). It is perplexing that Felski does not realize that the latter feeds the former, that is, that articulating this positive vision serves *as* a capitulation to conservative forces, which are after all the forces demanding that the humanities justify themselves in precisely those terms. I can only imagine that Felski has become so besotted with her characterization of the critic as the pompous, arrogant, relentlessly unpleasant-sounding avatar of "critiquiness," "an unmistakable blend of suspicion, self-confidence, and indignation" (187–188), that she feels that simply presenting a more likable stereotype of the English professor to the world will suddenly cause governors, state legislators, and Congress to allocate billions of dollars in funding for the humanities, as if publishing a number of less overtly political readings of this or that nineteenth-century novel in *New Literary History* will restore tenure-track positions to literature departments across the country. Of course, she and those whose voices hers joins in a groundswell do not truly believe such a thing, but they present (or market) their arguments as if they did.

Further, they do so with remarkable disingenuousness. For instance, as readers of his works know immediately, which is perhaps a sign that the postcritical critics assume that their audience has *not* done that reading, Felski's characterization of the critique-focused critic could not be more unlike Jameson himself, one of the most generous and careful readers around, who has always insisted that all texts have value and who finds utopian elements in even the most right-wing authors, such as the reactionary royalist Balzac or even the fascist Wyndham Lewis. By attacking Jameson, Marxist criticism, the hermeneutics of suspicion, and so on, these critics mischaracterize what is considered the "norm" in contemporary criticism and thus help to undermine the very humanities they claim to want to support. Regardless of intent, the postcritical project and others like it play right into the hands of the conservative political forces that have besieged higher education for the last 40 years or more.

Even if the surface reading movement, the postcritical approach, the digital humanities, or whatever adjacent scholarly practices were to be granted some status in the quest to help the humanities in a time when they are under siege by parsimonious administrations, hostile legislatures, a hard-hearted business "community," and rampant, cretinous anti-intellectualism, by effectively embracing the values of those enemies of the liberal arts, they already capitulate to the system those enemies have imposed, currently reinforce, and wish to perpetuate hereafter. I have no doubt, for instance, about Felski's good intentions when she claims in *The Limits of Critique* that her work "is motivated by a desire to articulate a positive vision for humanistic thought in the face of a growing skepticism about its value" (186). But this already demonstrates a willingness, if not a desire, to defer to those who do not value humanistic thought, and thus to allow the humanities in general to be redefined in order to accommodate their wishes. As Stanley Fish has argued,

> the demand for justification should be resisted because it is always the demand that you account for what you do in someone else's terms, be they the terms of the state, or of the economy, or of the project of democracy. "Tell me, why should I as a businessman or a governor or a preacher of the Word, value what you do?" There is no answer to this question that does not involve preferring the values of the person who asks it to yours. The moment you acquiesce to the demand for justification, you have lost the game, because even if you succeed, what you will have done is acknowledge that your efforts are instrumental to some external purpose; and if you fail, as is more likely, you leave yourself open to the conclusion that what you do is really not needed. The spectacle of departments of French or Byzantine Studies or Classics attempting to demonstrate that the state or society or the world order benefits from their existence is embarrassing and pathetic. These and other programs are in decline not because they have failed to justify themselves, but because they have tried to. ("Always Academicize")

The value of the literary humanities cannot be calculated in the terms set by those who oppose their very existence, and no matter how much one hopes to make the case for the inherently instrumental function of this work—Felski did give her earlier "manifesto" the title *Uses of Literature,* after all—we will never likely satisfy those among our friends and allies in other disciplines who favor utilitarian and quantitative measures of value; meanwhile, we will actively aid the enemies of the liberal arts in providing evidence of our unworthiness. There are some among those who lack imagination who need to be inspired, but there are others who would happily rid us all of the power of the imagination if they could.

It may well be that the postcritical turn in literary studies is itself a symptom of the broader neoliberalism permeating twenty-first-century society as a whole. Crystal Bartolovich has suggested, for example, that, "surface-reader appeals to the 'text itself' not only mark a pointed withdrawal from politics and theory but also—while humanities departments are contracting—internalize the economic imperative to scale back when we should be asserting the importance of humanistic inquiry to the most pressing problems facing our planet" (116). Lesjak sounds a similar note when observing, "the increasingly conservative mood within literary criticism and its key theoretical gestures," going on to say that, "[t]he overarching message seems to be: scale back, pare down, small aims met are better than grand ones unrealized, reclaim our disciplinary territory and hold on to it" (37). Moreover, Lesjak sees this as not only a politically questionable strategy, but as one that will certainly prove to be a failure in practice: if market demands require us to abandon critical theory and "return to our roots" in more simple forms of literary reading, as the argument goes,

> we can perhaps save our jobs as humanities professors by (cynically) complying with the instrumentalization of knowledge and thought driving the very institutional and university policies that see the humanities as obsolete... All this is done in the name of getting back to basics, while seemingly forgetting that we have been there before and that

it is no longer the place it used to be, if it ever was that place. (37)

The visions of austerity, modesty, and limited range fit well within an ideological system that imagines markets as operating efficiently, almost without the need for human actors or concerted efforts. It is not a great leap from allowing the texts to speak for themselves to leaving the market free to do its thing.

Robbins has identified another aspect of the postcritical approach's fundamentally neoliberal character. In eschewing those apparently politically charged approaches to the study of literature, including critique itself, such postcritical methods mirror the outwardly apolitical character of neoliberalism. As Robbins explains, "neoliberalism depoliticizes: It abandons to the silent authority of the market questions that had earlier been seen as requiring collective decision-making, which is to say matters of politics." In the specific case of academe, Robbins asserts, "[t]he 'new modesty' could never have gotten the attention it has if neoliberalism had not prepared the ground for it by undermining public funding for higher education, thereby ravaging the job market and demoralizing the job market's youngest victims, even the many today who face their situation and its necessarily more modest expectations with a cheerful, clear-eyed fatalism" ("Critical Correctness").

Neoliberal policies thus paved the way for postcritical literary studies, which in turn recapitulates the essential message of neoliberalism by allowing what had otherwise been understood to be political—works of literature and culture themselves, as well as the criticism used to help make sense of the ways those works help make sense of our world—to now appear to be largely devoid of, or at least set apart from, politics. To put it another way, by denying in advance any idea of a "political unconscious," and moreover by castigating or demonizing scholars for even attempting to seek such a thing in the first place, the postcritical critic reinforces the most basic tenet of neoliberal ideology, and does so in the most ideological manner possible: to wit, but insisting that this is the "natural" way of doing things.

There is yet another respect with which the postcritical form of literary criticism resembles and finds itself in league with neoliberal practices. In "Critical Correctness," Robbins points out that "[p]ostcritique, were it ever to be widely embraced, seems likely to produce a criticism that is closer to fandom. In lieu of critically examining literature or the culture it is a part of, postcritique encourages a rhetoric of helpful and largely positive advice to the would-be consumer." Appreciation of the text or author has always been an element of both teaching and research in academic literary studies, of course, but what has traditionally distinguished academic study from the more casual forms to be found in fan forums or reading groups is precisely the degree to which academic pedagogy and scholarship remains critical. To abandon critique will not restore university-level literary studies to some prelapsarian idyll about a time before critical theory, poststructuralism, or a hermeneutics of suspicion invaded English departments, but rather will emphasize the degree to which academic expertise of any kind is no longer necessary for marketing and selling the product.

In fact, although Robbins does not go this far, it seems to me that the advocates of surface reading, postcritique, or other such anti-interpretive approaches, perhaps unconsciously, have adopted a position enthusiastically taken by the managerial class of the neoliberal university: namely that students, as well as other readers, are fundamentally customers. As the consumerist ethos of postmodern fandom makes all too clear, the customer might relish limited forms of criticism, and often there's immense joy to be found in critically picking apart one's favorites texts, as any visit to a *Star Wars*, *Lord of the Rings*, or

Harry Potter discussion group will reveal almost instantly. But for the most part, those sorts of criticisms will function almost like surface readings, inasmuch as they must leave uncriticized the very conditions for the possibility or mode of production of the works under consideration.

At the very least, the fandom itself—along with ticket sales, merchandizing, and other branding possibilities—ensures that the ultimate beneficiaries of such "criticism" are the media conglomerates behind them. In Adorno and Horkheimer's day, what they called "the culture industry" appeared as a monumentally vast mystification machine, but our own era puts the old movie studio system and other such powers to shame when it comes to manipulating the tastes and spending habits of the public, both in the Americas and elsewhere around the world. The entertainment industry now is branded in such a way that fans cheer as much for the franchises and the corporations as they do for their favorite characters, texts, and authors. And, as Gerry Canavan has pointed out in "Disney's Endgame," there are fewer and fewer players in that sport. Of the 20 highest grossing Hollywood films in the past decade (i.e., 2010–2019), all were sequels or part of a larger franchise, and 18 were produced by a single corporate entity, The Walt Disney Company, which now controls Lucasfilm, Pixar, and the Marvel Studios, along with *The Simpsons*. In a field in which postcritical commentary replaces interpretation and critique, fandom is likely to become more and more seen as the appropriate way to examine cultural artifacts like films or novels, in which case academic literary criticism may suffer the fate of serious cultural journalism in an era of sponsored content and infomercials, which is to say, it will still exist, but it will become much harder to find. It may disappear entirely from higher education. The panegyricists of "attachment" and "affect" may well find themselves unwittingly advertising the Disney Channel or its various affiliates across media platforms as they plump for anti-interpretive or postcritical approaches to literature.

Postcritique as Ideology

There is another profoundly pernicious and duplicitous aspect to the postcritical position. While claiming a certain sort of populism, and in particular assuming a stance in defense of the common or "lay" reader, Felski would seem to be supporting a general movement against experts and expertise. "Ordinary" language, after all, is for the most part defined by its difference from the technical vocabularies of experts. The postcritical movement in twentieth-century literary studies offers aid and comfort to those who would support further adjunctification within higher education, or the broader deprofessionalization of various fields (medicine, law, accounting, and so on) in society at large. If "lay readers" and "ordinary people" are just as capable of "reading" as professionally trained and educated literary critics—or if, indeed, as Felski suggests, they are actually *better* at doing so than the professionals, who are somehow blinded by their paranoid or suspicious minds—then why on earth should we have such professionals teaching literature? Wholly apart from, but undoubtedly still related to, economic considerations, would it not be preferable to employ university-level teachers without having to countenance all that superfluous, expensive, and apparently unnecessary training? Of course, many if not most adjunct faculty members *do* have as much training as their increasingly small number of tenured or tenure-track colleagues, but the point is that they will be treated—and above all *paid*—as if they did not.

Outside of academe, such deprofessionalization has also been happening at an alarming rate, consistent with neoliberal capitalist and managerial practices aimed at lowering costs, increasing "efficiency" (apologies, but that term almost always requires scare-quotes in such circumstances), and so on. Nurses, paramedics, and even technicians are frequently called upon to do more and more of what medical doctors had previously devoted themselves to performing, for example. Similarly, law clerks, paralegals, and even legal software may now be tasked with the duties of a lawyer, and a single attorney may be able to "sign off on" the work done by hordes of non-lawyers employed by the firm. Likewise "tax-preparers," along with other financial services personnel and also computer programs, replace certified public accountants who would have required a great deal of formal training and certification. Much of this is also outsourced entirely, so the work may not even take place in the company itself. The trends toward deprofessionalization and outsourcing have been steadily increasing in recent decades, and it is probably not merely coincidental that these trends have accelerated when greater numbers of women or minorities have entered those very professions. In many respects, a discourse or rhetoric favoring the "average" or "common" reader contributes to this process, which inevitably drives down wages and benefits for those workers, even as this ideology's proponents laud the victims of such policies for their purportedly greater authenticity and authority.

However, ironically perhaps, the model of postcritical reading also favors an aristocracy of very highly placed critics who are empowered to call out their well-trained foes while nominally supporting the commoner. One sees this especially in Felski's own style of writing, which features the sort of *ex cathedra* pronouncements that must be accepted by all. What I refer to is her habit of asserting otherwise contested or even dubious claims without citation or explanation, relying upon her own authority and considerable professional prestige to justify it. Thus, for example, in speaking of a memoir by Eva Hoffman, Felski writes "[w]hile nostalgia often gets a bad press in the humanities, *Lost in Translation* purposively dwells on the affective force of what it means to be tied to a country and a language" (*Hooked*, 151). The inelegance of the phrasing aside

(Felski seems to have conflated the ordinary phrases "getting bad press" with "getting a bad rap"), the first clause only makes sense if the reader implicitly trusts Felski's total knowledge of "the humanities" and *their* characteristic and generalizable beliefs. At no point will Felski ever provide even a single example of a critic in the humanities who expresses disdain for "nostalgia," and I suspect many literature students and even seasoned experts would, if called upon to do so, struggle to find their own examples. If they could think of examples, it might still be hard to see those as representative of "the humanities" as a whole. Those of us who have known the long and august history of "nostalgia" as a crucial literary concept—from Homer's original tale of Odysseus's homecoming (i.e., his *nostos*) to Don Quixote's longing for a chivalric world no longer present, through the pervasive influence of Romanticism on modern literature and critical theory, to Walter Benjamin's inventive forms of critical nostalgia and on to the pervasive uses of memory and longing in terms of place and time in diaspora writings and postcolonial theory—will question whether we are allowed to balk at a dictum that is so obviously false. Felski asserts this truly dubious idea with such casual assurance, and indeed with such an air of being infallibly correct, as to not feel the need to introduce or justify it with evidence, that her readers are almost literally cowed into taking it for Gospel truth.

In criticizing Felski's characterization of mainstream academic critics (or the persona she names *critique*) as ones who "look down on" literature, who imagine themselves as being "superior" to the writers or texts in question, and so on, I once pointed out that I could think of no critic who actually did that, and Felski in *The Limits of Critique* provides little evidence herself. A graduate student I know said that he did not think Felski needed to do so, since it was so "obvious" that that is what critics do. I asked, well, can you name the critics who are doing that, maybe citing the actual words from their books or essays in which they show themselves to be "looking down on" the texts they read? I have no doubt that, with a thorough search, we could have found some instance or other in which that had happened, but none sprang to mind right away, and certainly we could get no sense that it would be so widespread and taken for granted as to be considered the "norm" in academic literary criticism *tout court*.

Hence, the effect of this overgeneralizing and straw-man argumentation is to perpetuate a fundamental ideological condition, setting up the "ordinary" lay reader as the more authentic consumer of literary art, while firmly ensconcing a mere handful of elite experts as the supreme authority over the understanding and appreciation of such art. If ideology can be defined, as it sometimes has been, as a means of presenting socially constructed phenomena as if they were purely natural, then we can see that the postcritical approach to literature becomes an ideology in its own right. (Indeed, in *The Limits of Critique*, Felski includes a section in which she defends "the natural" against the antinaturalism of suspicious critics [69–81].) Felski need not offer specific examples of objectionable practices by critics or other writers, using quotations or other traditional tools of the literary critical trade, for she can simply pronounce from her exalted position as a postcritical critic what is and what is not happening, as if such things were not contested or subject to change.

In this manner, the foremost proponent of postcritique sometime comes off sounding like the aristocrat who seems to advocate for the *hoi polloi* while actually ensuring that her position of unquestioned authority remains secure. I am not speaking of Felski's actual professional positions, which certainly are prestigious—a named professorship at a major, nationally recognized research university, alongside the Niels Bohr Professorship at a prominent university in Denmark, formerly the editor of an influential academic journal, and so forth—but of her generally exalted place in academic literary criticism. Not that she would agree with his argument, but Fish infamously remarked, in response to a question of how he could be sure that his interpretation of a given text was accurate, "Because I am Stanley Fish, I teach at Johns Hopkins University, and I make seventy-five thousand dollars a year. That's why" (see Olson 162; the salary is in 1970s dollars, of course.) Seemingly crass, Fish's point is related to his view of the "interpretive communities" which lend authority to, and thereby do much to instantiate the accepted "truth" of, a given interpretation. That is, if a highly paid English professor at one of the most well-respected universities in the country affirms a given interpretation as accurate, then it will thereby be invested with an authority supplied by the institutional and professional matrices in which such interpretations would emerge. As an antifoundationalist, Fish would never assert that there could be any absolute and unchanging "true" interpretation (and he rightly doubts that foundationalists could credibly produce one either), but he assures his audience that this cannot lead to an "anything goes," semantic anarchy, since the "interpretative community"—here, English literature scholars, most of them within the academy—will place limits on the range of acceptable meanings (see, e.g., his *Is There a Text in This Class?* 335–336). But, as I say, the upshot of this apparently reasonable notion is that professional credentialing and prestige has more to do with what readings are considered acceptable or correct than any methodological or analytical practice.

I suspect that the authority to attack critique, nominally in favor of the more honest and wholesome interpretive (or anti-interpretative) practices of the putatively "ordinary" reader, derives much of its force from the elite position within the very institutions of academic literary criticism that Felski, Best, Marcus, and others are criticizing. If in their critique of the hermeneutics of suspicion, *they* effectively say that there is nothing to see here, please move along, then many beginning students, along to many less decorated critics, emergent scholars, similarly situated fellow elites, or other readers will be apt to fall into line. All the more so considering, as befits an ideological program of this sort, postcritique or surface reading presents itself as the less elitist, more demotic practice. The most authoritative authorities thus give sanction to the putatively less authoritative perspectives, all the while supporting (perhaps unconsciously) the very institutional forces that would delegitimize and defund the very field in which they would operate.

The Dialectic of Utopia and Ideology

To return to the Jameson quotation with which I began, critical interpretation and analysis is needed precisely because "no society has ever been quite so mystified in quite so many ways as our own, saturated as it is with messages and information, the very vehicles of mystification," and this is far truer today than it was in 1981 when *The Political Unconscious* was published. The various forms of literary criticism aiming to counter or avoid the hermeneutics of suspicion are both symptoms of and contributors to that pervasive mystification. In the final chapter of that monumental study, Jameson insisted that critics be attuned to what he referred to as "the dialectic of utopia and ideology," which for him meant that while all texts are necessarily and inescapably ideological (hence, "negative" in the parlance of the postcritical critics), they also contain or embody elements of a legitimately utopian (hence, "positive") impulse or quality in the form of some kind of class consciousness. There, as elsewhere, Jameson insists that every proper *critique* must pay attention to both the positive and the negative aspects of its object. In Jameson's words, "any Marxist analysis of culture…can no longer be content with its demystifying vocation to unmask and to demonstrate the ways in which a cultural artifact fulfills a specific ideological mission," but must also seek "to project its simultaneously Utopian power as the symbolic affirmation of a specific historical and class form of collective unity" (291). These are not two alternative perspectives, Jameson avers, but rather they constitute a unified point of view in which both are always and already present at the same time.

Jameson is here talking about the power of Marxist literary criticism, with its profoundly sensitive method of ideology critique, to inform our understanding of narratives and their relationship to our social, political, and historical experience more broadly. But this is also the crux of Marxism itself, which requires us as part of our *praxis* to be able to critically interpret the world in order to open up the space for, and keep alive the promise of, changing the world. As Jameson explained in *Valences of the Dialectic*,

> [a] Marxist politics is a Utopian project or program for transforming the world, and replacing a capitalist mode of production with a radically different one. But it is also a conception of historical dynamics in which it is posited that the whole new world is also objectively in emergence all around us, without our necessarily at once perceiving it; so that alongside our conscious praxis and our strategies for producing change, we may also take a more receptive and interpretive stance in which, with the proper instruments and registering apparatus, we may detect the allegorical stirrings of a different state of things, the imperceptible and even immemorial ripenings of the seeds of time, the subliminal and subcutaneous eruptions of whole new forms of life and social relations. (416)

Interpretation, in literary studies more broadly, certainly should not stop at finding "the" single, discrete "Truth" (with a capital *T*), a Grail unworthy of the quest even if it somehow actually existed. But a robust critical hermeneutic is needed to make sense of the present, situating it in relation to the historical past no longer within our grasp, which in turn is a prerequisite for any meaningful change in our futures, even if what is at stake is only the institutional future of higher education and not our collective future within a mode of production whose aim is to destroy us and the earth in short order. At least when it comes to the more modest practice of reading works of literature, the results would be not only "truer" in that ironic, Nietzschean sense, but also more interesting. And therein lies the ultimate sin of surface reading, the postcritical approach, or whatever: in their boundless mystification they are undoubtedly making our literature, as well as our lives, a good deal less interesting and arguably less safe.

Chapter 3

Critique Unlimited

In recent years, whether having to do with the generally perceived crisis in the humanities or with some more basic upheaval in education, the value and function of literary criticism has been increasingly called into question. Leaving aside the hue and cry over the decline in the numbers of humanities and literature majors, not to mention the various pronouncements of new forms of cultural illiteracy in a supposed post-literate society, criticism itself has come under fire as a somehow illegitimate or flawed practice. Academic literary critics are viewed as hopelessly out of touch with some imagined "mainstream" reading public, a view that has become a cornerstone of a cultural journalism bent on toppling university-based intellectuals from their ostensible pedestals. Some of these assaults on the ivory tower have been launched by academics themselves, many of whom express nostalgia for some prelapsarian moment when the study of literature was somehow unsullied by "theory," and equally academic literary critics have proposed solutions that would in one way or another help to save the humanities.

Among the more celebrated recent examples of this, Rita Felski's call for a "postcritical" approach to literature is, in her own words, "motivated by a desire to articulate a positive vision for humanistic thought in the face of growing skepticism about its value" (*Limits of Critique* 186). The object of Felski's polemic is something she calls *critique*, which for her is as much a rhetorical attitude or tone as a methodology or genre. As she sees it, critique is inextricably tied to the "hermeneutics of suspicion," a term borrowed from Paul Ricoeur and used to designate an approach to interpretation that seeks to unmask meanings hidden from the everyday reader. In Ricoeur's characterization, "[t]his hermeneutics is not an explication of the object, but a tearing off of masks, an interpretation that reduces disguise"(*Freud and Philosophy* 30). Felski does not go into Ricoeur's argument beyond repeatedly citing the phrase, but she asserts that this hermeneutics of suspicion lies at the heart of the problem with literary studies as currently practiced. Although her target is explicitly critique, Felski implicitly mounts an argument against literary or critical theory as well. Even as she good-naturedly confesses to having dabbled in theory herself, she clearly sees "Theory-with-a-capital *T*" as abetting the critical attitude she opposes. Against appearances, Felski asserts that her book is "not conceived as a polemic against critique," and she admits that her, "previous writing (in feminist theory and cultural studies, among other topics) owes an extended debt to critical thinking. I was weaned on the Frankfurt School and still get a kick out of teaching Foucault" (5). As such, her polemic against critique and against a certain hermeneutics of suspicion offers a good example of the current, widespread antipathy toward theory in the literary humanities today.

That a certain "antitheory" sensibility pervades literary studies at present is not really in doubt, and I believe that the turn away from theory in recent years, like and also related to the turn away from ideology critique discussed in the last chapter, has had deleterious effects for literary criticism as a whole. The current trend toward postcritical approaches to literature is itself part of the movement away from theory, inasmuch as the principal theoretical traditions imagined by the postcritical critics have tended to trace their pedigrees back to that unholy trinity of Marx, Nietzsche, and Freud, those "masters of suspicion," as Ricoeur dubbed them, whose later twentieth- and twenty-first-century legatees have included a pantheon (or is it a pandemonium?) of celebrated critical theorists, such as Walter Benjamin, Georg Lukács, Antonio Gramsci, the Frankfurt School researchers, Jacques Lacan, Michel Foucault, Gilles Deleuze, Jacques Derrida, Fredric Jameson, Gayatri Spivak, Judith Butler, the other poststructuralists, and the postmodernists, and so on. The writings of Marx, Nietzsche, and Freud alone represent an astonishing diversity of thought, and the idea that the wide-ranging theoretical traditions made possible by their work could be neatly encapsulated into a single critical program or agenda is absurd, but one feature these profound heterogenous discourses share is an apparent commitment to question, to look into more deeply or to look beyond the world as it presents itself to us. In this sense, critical theory is subversive, not so much in terms of a political project and in the more literal or etymological sense that theory attempts to undermine and overturn the *status quo*.

Not surprisingly, then, an effect if not the aim of a lot of the polemics against critical theory has been to support a *status quo*, or in some more reactionary cases a *status quo ante*, that theory and critique were to have unfairly maligned. Indeed, as I have said, the postcritical and antitheoretical tendencies in contemporary academic literary studies are symptomatic of a greater capitulation to what has been thought of as neoliberalism in higher education, which has involved a consumerist ethos and a degradation of thinking in all corners of its fields of influence. By trying to appeal to a public discourse fundamentally at odds with criticism and theory—that is, a discourse wholly committed to perpetuating a certain order of things and to limiting both the critique thereof and speculation over alternatives—the postcritical and antitheoretical scholars have ceded the territory to the enemy, allowing the opponents of literature and the humanities to set the terms of the debate, which has in turn frequently presented a crassly utilitarian or pragmatist vision of literary and cultural studies. I find a curious resonance between the contemporary critique of critical theory and the jeremiads emerging from the culture wars in higher education in the

1980s, and I maintain that a robust critical theory and practice is all the more necessary to combat the forces arrayed against the humanities in the twenty-first century. Moreover, I assert that such critical theory and practice is the very *raison d'etre* for the humanities.

In discussing these matters, I have tried to succumb neither to feelings of nostalgia nor to those of resignation. That is, notwithstanding the fantastic critical utopias that epigones like myself might envision as existing in the heyday of our heroes and heroines of yore, it is clear that there was never really a historical Golden Age of theory to which we should strive to return. As I discuss below, there really was no heyday of theory, in academe or in the society at large, even if there had been various moments of excitement and possibility along the way. Similarly, there is not much of value in the all-too-commonly-held sense that "*plus ça change, plus c'est la même chose,*" despite the nagging aura of *déjà vu* that accompanies any retrospective analysis of the phenomenon. The narrative of critical theory's rise and fall in the literary humanities does not maintain a simple or linear plot, although various versions of the story can be told with different aims and effects. Similarly, the diversity of literary criticism and theory assures the possibility that many excellent and many awful works can be produced and coexist, with an extraordinarily wide range of examples along the spectrum. In this chapter, I want to address first antitheory itself, then its current expression in what is today celebrated as a postcritical approach to literature, and finally what I suggest is our duty, as culture workers in the literary humanities, to oppose this vision.

The Persistence of Antitheory

Decrying the lingering critical attitude she associates mainly with poststructuralism, Felski points out that, "While the era of Theory with a capital *T* is now more or less over, this same disposition remains widely in force, carried over into the scrutiny of particular historical or textual artifacts" (25). Felski's sense that theory's epoch has ended is quite common nowadays, even as the formal remnants of the era are everywhere to be seen. Indeed, I have often thought that the so-called "death of theory" was due, in part and paradoxically, to what could be thought of as theory's huge success. That is, what had once been considered somewhat arcane types of critical theory became so much an intrinsic and familiar part of the study of literature, and of other subjects as well, that it lost a great deal of its critical power, a power based to a significant degree on its fundamental alterity or strangeness as a discourse and as a set of practices. To employ an overused term these days, theory became normalized, such that it was no longer *outré*, radical, or unorthodox, but had become an ordinary aspect of literary studies, if not a new orthodoxy, to be sure.

In my own department, at a university originally founded as a regional teachers' college, our undergraduate students are required to take a course called "Critical Theory for English Majors," and our Masters literature students take a similar graduate-level course titled simply "Literary Scholarship." Several professors who teach these courses "do" theory in their own scholarly activities, and we have had on our faculty a professor expressly hired as a specialist in literary criticism and theory since 2002. I think it is fair to say that these are not eccentric practices at universities and English departments around the United States. Apparently, by our own reckoning, the students majoring in English must have some basic familiarity with theory, even if courses on Shakespeare, Milton, and Chaucer are not required. That a faculty like ours in a time like ours feels the need to maintain a theory requirement is, I think, a sign that yesteryear's *avant-garde* proponents of critical theory—the Yale Critics, Colin MacCabe, the Marxist Literary Group, or other embattled partisans from the 1970s—sort of "won." (In *Beginning Theory*, for example, Peter Barry sketched a history of theory's rise and fall using ten signature events, including "the MacCabe Affair" [i.e., the controversial decision by Cambridge not to promote then-lecturer Colin MacCabe, who was apparently tainted by his associations with structuralist theory], to mark various moments along the way.) In this sense, theory is everywhere in the academic study of literature today.

However, one could probably argue with equal force that the addition of theory courses to a standard English curriculum is a sign of just how much theorists and theory have "lost" over the years. For while courses like these do acquaint students with names like Saussure, Derrida, Lacan, and Foucault, they could also rob such theorists of any transformative power, as they become keywords in an informal disciplinary lexicon, and their work reduced to simplistic exercises designed to be readily grasped by undergraduates in order to demonstrate basic proficiency. Students learn that there is no meaningful difference between performing a feminist reading of a given text, a deconstruction of it, or a Marxist analysis; these are merely different critical "lenses" one may choose to look through when reading. Notoriously, in fact, in their attention to formal features, meticulous detail, and close reading, deconstructive analyses often resemble the New Critical interpretations of old, which might help to explain its prominence among Yale critics weaned on William K. Wimsatt and Cleanth Brooks. Students may now incorporate terms like *signifier*, *hegemony*, *the Other*, or *performativity* into vocabularies once featuring *allegory*, *irony*, or *symbolism* as keywords, but the basic approach to the materials remains pretty much the same. That is assuming that attention to form and to interpretation is being done at all.

The basic story told about the rise of theory in literary studies is widely accepted, at least judging from the many textbooks designed for use in courses such as our "Critical Theory for English Majors." The narrative tells of a prehistoric time—actually, merely the pre-1960s—when a hegemonic New Criticism (especially in the USA) or a sort of Leavisite humanism (if we are talking about the UK) held sway over all approaches to literature. That these informal schools of criticism themselves represented *theories*, that they were also quite innovative and controversial, and that there was significant resistance to them within both the groves of academe and the wider literary world are seldom mentioned in the introductions to literary or critical theory. The advent of "theory" is depicted as part of a general backlash against New Criticism or liberal humanism, a backlash occasioned mainly by the incursion of foreign thought and of different disciplines into literature departments in the 1960s and 1970s. French structuralism brought Saussurean linguistics to bear on not only literary texts, but on texts across the social and cultural domains; after all, with semiotics, everything can become a sign-system to be decoded or a text to be interpreted, as Roland Barthes displayed so elegantly with such books as *Mythologies* and *The Fashion System*. Along those same Francophone lines, works of and figures representing anthropology (Lévi-Strauss), psychology (Lacan), philosophy (Foucault, Deleuze, Derrida, Althusser, Lyotard), history (Foucault again), sociology (Bourdieu), and other disciplinary fields insinuated themselves into the required reading lists of literature scholars. Add to this a Germanic tradition, deriving from Marx, Nietzsche, and Freud, if not also Hegel and Kant, which—along with Georg Lukács, Martin Heidegger, Walter Benjamin, and the Frankfurt School, among others—led to various schools of theory mingling with or contesting these others. And apart from the foreign invaders, a certain home-grown sensibility among English professors led them to develop critiques of New Criticism or old-fashioned humanism on their own, owing to a variety of political or intellectual motives.

The key to the story is rebellion against an ostensibly dogmatic norm, in which the proponents of theory are cast as revolutionaries, but to those who spent any time investigating the history of criticism this narrative never really rang true. For one thing, there was plenty of "theory" before the New Criticism or its detractors. A parochial focus on English, as opposed to other languages and literatures, is partly to blame, as the New Criticism was never particularly influential on scholars in, say, French or German departments, where phenomenological and philological approaches, including "style studies," were more commonly practiced in the 1950s. As for what would come to be called interdisciplinarity, certainly T. S. Eliot or F. R. Leavis read widely in philosophy, history, and other disciplinary fields, and even the most provincial of English professors read works from different languages. To the extent that what becomes known as *theory* develops out of literary and philosophical traditions or counter-traditions of the nineteenth century, as Andrew Cole has discussed in *The Birth of Theory*, even such early critics as I. A. Richards or R. P. Blackmur were obviously already engaged in theory. Moreover, major figures who do not fit neatly within this now dominant story—I am thinking of Edmund Wilson, Kenneth Burke, or Northrop Frye, for instance—are often omitted entirely. If an important early study like Frank Lentricchia's *After the New Criticism* (1980) helped to establish the rise of theory as a reaction to the New Criticism's less obviously theoretical approach, the textbook history of this intellectual trajectory by later scholars neglected Lentricchia's emphasis on Frye, Burke, and Kermode, as well as his discussions of existentialism, phenomenology, and an American Studies that frequently eschewed any contact with the fallacies associated with the New Criticism. In fact, when it came to American literature, the predominance of what came to be known as the Myth and Symbol school of criticism ensured that a very different sort of theoretical framework influenced generations of scholars in that field. The commonly understood narrative of the emergence and dissemination of theory that is presented in so many introductory guides involves a great deal of overgeneralization and oversimplification at best.

It is also the case that the resistance to theory has been part and parcel of the rise of theory, with scholars and critics pooh-poohing the various schools of theory almost as quickly as they became known, almost literally so in the case of Frederick Crews' *The Pooh Perplex,* originally published in 1963 and lampooning Marxist, Freudian, Mythic, New Critical, and other forms of literary criticism, which remains a classic touchstone in this regard; nearly 4 decades later, Crews published *Postmodern Pooh,* in which he satirizes various approaches (deconstruction, feminism, postcolonial studies, etc.) to have emerged in academic literary studies since the 1960s. A symbol of this overlap between theory and antitheory may be found in the coincidence of Stephen Knapp and Walter Benn Michaels's notorious "Against Theory" article and Terry Eagleton's bestselling *Literary Theory: An Introduction,* published within a year of each other in 1982–1983. The latter became a classroom staple—still widely available, now in a third edition—that has introduced more than one generation to the subject, doing more than its share in helping theory to become an essential part of literary studies, while the former argued that literary criticism and scholarship would be better off without theory entirely.

My own experience with theory was more subtle. Influenced by my adolescent enthusiasm for existentialism, for the fiction of Jean-Paul Sartre and Albert Camus, but especially for the ideas of Marx, Nietzsche, and Freud—I was already inclined toward those "masters of suspicion" apparently—I majored in philosophy while remaining keenly interested in literature, especially nineteenth- and twentieth-century European literature. (William Faulkner was, in my sophomoric opinion, among the only acceptable US writers, but mostly because I viewed him as an American Dostoevsky.) In my first semester in college, I took a course in Comparative Literature taught by a professor from the German department and called "The Poetics of Thought," which focused on texts that combined the literary and the philosophical. It was not a theory course, and Erich Auerbach was perhaps the only twentieth-century critic directly mentioned in class, but it was this sort of mélange of philosophy and literature that excited me the most. I did not realize that such a blend, when examined critically and perhaps with more focus on language itself, was affiliated with what was being called *theory*, and I was especially ignorant of what might be more narrowly understood as *literary theory*. Given the writers I was most interested in, the theory produced seemed to be far less a rejection of this or that dominant practice within a disciplinary field than a continuation of what might be considered interdisciplinary tendencies within literature and philosophy broadly conceived. I ended up focusing within my philosophy major on post-Kantian Continental thought, and I took as many courses in the Literature program (but not English, incidentally) as I did in my major: between the two departments of philosophy and literature, I took entire courses on Hegel, Marx and Marxism, Nietzsche, Freud, the Frankfurt School, Lacan, Foucault, Deleuze, and modern social theory including works by Lukács, Gramsci, Strauss, and Habermas. By the time I neared graduation and applied for graduate schools, I knew that I wanted to "do" theory.

And so I did. I arrived in a graduate program already known for its commitments to literary and cultural theory (e.g., the doctoral program based in the Department of English at the University of Pittsburgh was then, and is now still, called the "PhD in Critical and Cultural Studies"), and I was thrilled to study under professors whose own work represented both the study and practice of theory. Clearly, I was in the right place at the right time! Imagine my surprise, consternation, and perhaps disappointment, then, when in my first year my own advisor, Paul A. Bové, published a book called *In the Wake of*

Theory, whose opening line read as follows: "During the late 1970s and the 1980s, various political, cultural, and intellectual forces combined to bring the moment of 'literary theory' to an end in the United States" (1). Wait, I thought, theory is over? I just got here. And *wait*, theory was over way back in the early 1980s, before I even went to college? The "wake of theory" phrase itself suggested the dual meaning of a requiem and an aftermath or lingering influence, but whichever metaphor was preferred, clearly Bové was saying that theory itself had to be understood as a thing of the past.

Bové's book was a response to what he took to be a dominant, antitheory discourse in both the academy and the broader public sphere during that decade, more or less tied to a sort of generalized Reaganism and Thatcherism, combined with a crassly pragmatic or professionalized view of the value of higher education. Within academic literary criticism, not only had the old guard who had withstood the encroachments of Continental theory onto the territory of English literature (say, an M. H. Abrams) effectively maintained their opposition to theory, but a forcefully articulated antitheory position was stressed by some of the young Turks of literary academe as well: I have mentioned Stephen Knapp and Walter Benn Michaels's famous "Against Theory" article in *Critical Inquiry* in 1982, which made the bizarre, neopragmatist argument that meaning and intention, language and speech acts, and knowledge and belief were each inseparable. The bizarreness of this "pragmatism" did not go unnoticed, as even W. J. T. Mitchell, in introducing the debate stirred up by this article, noted with irony that nobody in practice, but only "in theory," could buy Knapp's and Michaels's conclusion, since, for example, "in practice, to say I *believe* something to be the case is tantamount to saying that I do not *know* it for a fact" (*Against Theory* 9).

Worse still, major theorists themselves appeared to be turning away from "theory," as when Edward W. Said criticized

"American Left Criticism" or "Traveling Theory" in *The World, the Text, and the Critic,* among others of his post-*Orientalism* writings, or later when such eminent figures as Lentricchia (whose *After the New Criticism* and *Criticism and Social Change* constituted major studies of, and contributions to, literary theory), Stanley Fish, Harold Bloom, Henry Louis Gates Jr., and Stephen Greenblatt all abandoned theory in favor of this or that largely antitheoretical form of rhetorical, historical, cultural studies, or, in Lentricchia's particular case, fiction writing.

Outside the ivory tower, the outsized influence of William Bennett's "To Reclaim a Legacy" report—since when does a National Endowment for the Humanities report make national news?—and bestsellers like Allan Bloom's *The Closing of the American Mind* or E. D. Hirsch's *Cultural Literacy* proved that there was a market for such reactionary responses to theory. (It almost makes one nostalgic to recall that Bloom identified "the Nietzscheanization of the Left" as the chief malady of the era; if only US conservatives today prescribed reading more Plato as the cure to what ails the national culture!) Conservatives in the media, such as George Will, Lynn Cheney, Pat Buchanan, and William Safire, lapped this stuff up, and they made sure to keep the public apprised of the baleful consequences of theory on higher education and Western civilization more generally in Op-Ed pages and news talk shows. As more books followed, such as Roger Kimball's *Tenured Radicals* and Dinesh D'Souza's *Illiberal Education,* to name just two influential ones, even the liberal media jumped in, all too eager to cherry-pick titles from the Modern Language Association's annual convention program, for instance, to show how dangerous and out-of-touch humanities professors were. In most cases, the problem with those professors was related to, if not identified simply as, their embrace of theory, such that terms like Marxist, feminist, "deconstructionist," and postmodernist came to serve as ready-made labels with which to dismiss any academic critic with whom one had problems. In 1992, antitheory already seemed to be mainstream, theory itself in retreat if not defeated outright, and Bové's eulogistic assessment of theory's gains necessarily included a sense that literary criticism itself was no longer critical.

This brief, oversimplified rehearsal merely serves to emphasize the profoundly antitheoretical intellectual and professional contexts in which many scholars in the humanities first came to theory. Antitheory has been dominant throughout, and yet theory's influence on a certain sort of critical discourse, as well as its value as a commodity, remains fairly strong. One of the reasons antitheory maintains its prestige, after all, is that it can so potently convince others that theory is still an enemy worthy of vanquishing. Theory may well be a straw man in these arguments, but it is a very resilient one.

The Postcritical Turn

Much like the culture warriors of the 1980s, today all manner of scholars stand heroically against theory, as if by doing so they have already demonstrated themselves to be heroic. They are "saving" literature from the barbarians, or perhaps they are saving literature from the hegemonic elites on behalf of those unfairly dismissed as barbaric themselves. By denouncing critical theory, it seems, such critics claim to be rescuing the field from itself. One of the more celebrated challenges within the literary humanities comes from the postcritical approach to the study of literature, an approach championed by Felski in her book *The Limits of Critique*. Felski, who has said that her position is part of a "growing groundswell of voices" (given their abundance in her writing, mixed metaphors may well be a stylistic feature of postcritique), but she has stood out, making the news both for her provocative arguments and for becoming the recipient of a multimillion-dollar grant, which has been awarded to her to support her investigation into various postcritical ways of studying literature. The *Chronicle of Higher Education* even published an advertisement for her work masquerading as an article titled "What's Wrong with Literary Studies?," in which Felski was specifically presented as not just the person to answer the question—the subtitle's answer: "the field has become cynical and paranoid"—but also as the one to make literary studies "right" again. Citing with approval the argument of her book about the odiousness of critique and also endorsing the broader notion of a postcritical project as the salvation of literary studies today, the author Marc Parry begins and ends with references to her $4.2 million grant, almost as if the dollar-amount of the award reinforces the value of the postcritical approach to literature.

Being opposed to critique is extraordinarily lucrative, it seems, and those of us trained in "the hermeneutics of suspicion" are likely not surprised. Felski herself has hijacked this felicitous phrase normally attributed to Ricoeur, used by him to characterize the interpretative strategies of Marx, Nietzsche, and Freud, but Felski does not go on to analyze the term or to discuss the writings of these masters of suspicion. In fact, she simply invokes the label, out of context and certainly without reference to Ricoeur's own more particular uses of the term *suspicion*, as a way of characterizing the sorts of literary criticism she now opposes in *The Limits of Critique*. In *Freud and Philosophy*, Ricoeur had distinguished the interpretative strategies of the "school of suspicion" from those of what he acknowledges would be a school of "faith." (As it happens, Ricoeur does not actually use the literal phrase "hermeneutics of suspicion" in that book.) In this schema, the faithful interpreter seeks to recover a lost meaning in the text, whereas the suspicious interpreter doubts the existence of the pure meaning, instead looking at the ways that the text disguises or masks the truth. Although Felski never admits it, Ricoeur's position vis-à-vis the "masters of suspicion" is largely one of admiration. Whereas

Felski sees critique as being undergirded by a rhetoric and tone of cynicism, Ricoeur expressly states that, "[t]hese three masters of suspicion are not to be misunderstood, however, as three masters of skepticism...All three clear the horizon for a more authentic word, for a new reign of Truth, not only by means of a 'destructive' critique, but the invention of an art of *interpreting*" (33). This more appreciative view of Marx, Nietzsche, and Freud as inventors of interpretive arts is nevertheless wholly consistent with Felski's more dismissive view of these theorists, since part of her opposition to critique can also be understand as merely anti-interpretation. In fact, her objection to the "hermeneutics of suspicion" and to the theoretical and critical traditions that are indebted to the writings of these masters of suspicion may have more to do with the "hermeneutics" than with the suspiciousness. In this way, her interests diverge quite significantly from Ricoeur's concerns.

Felski's actual opponent, however, is not any particular critic who claims membership in the school of suspicion. The reader of *The Limits of Critique* will search in vain for what surely must have been the missing section in which Felski engages with a specific work of criticism, showing how its rhetoric and tone belied its baleful project of undermining literary art in favor of demonstrating that particular reader's inherent superiority to the texts and its would-be admirers. Much as she paraphrases or imagines critics making suspicious arguments about cultural artifacts, Felski does not really present a clear example of a critic or work of criticism to support the argument. The closest thing I could find to such an example was a short paragraph, no more than half a page, summarizing Jameson's *The Political Unconscious*. As a Marxist critic who draws upon both psychoanalytic theory and Nietzschean critique of ethics to make the case for a new approach to interpreting literary texts in such a way as to reveal hidden ideological or political content in the forms, Jameson would seem to be the natural target, if not the poster-child, for Felski's criticism, and indeed she does cite Jameson's famous text as an exemplary case. (Of course, one obvious objection to employing *The Political Unconscious* as a cautionary example of critique's hegemony within literary and cultural studies in the present is its age. Can we really say that a book published in 1981, no matter how influential, represents the dominant critical ethos of academic literary studies today?) But even so, the best Felski can muster in her critique of that work—beyond summarizing it, which I suppose counts as criticism, assuming one is preaching to the well-read choir—is the vague suggestion that Jameson is insufficiently "respectful, even reverential" toward the texts, and that he does not make a "good-faith effort to draw out a text's implicit meanings" (57). I would argue that this is a misreading of Jameson, who makes no moral judgments whatsoever about the texts and is remarkably sensitive to the aesthetic appeal of literature, not only in *The Political Unconscious* (with its meticulous and sensitive readings of novels by Balzac, Gissing, and Conrad, for example) but throughout his career. That said, of course, Jameson's commitments to critical theory certainly place him at odds with Felski's postcritical approach.

In fact, Felski's choice to focus on such nebulous forms as the *rhetoric*, *tone*, or *mood* of critique, as opposed to working through various examples of actual critical readings with which she takes issue, makes it rather difficult to grapple with her argument at a substantive level. The would-be champions of critique find themselves in a position somewhat like that of Bové in the 1980s, who lamented his inability to engage critically with Bloom's *The Closing of the American Mind* because, as he put it, "[t]he book appears as a set of mere assertions about other books and events whose authority must simply be granted to Bloom"; Bové goes on to say that "the book appears everywhere and always to be made up of gross simplifications" (69). As a critic herself and a literature scholar, Felski knows much better, but it is also true that *The Limits of Critique* sometimes reads like a rambling polemic against largely unnamed straw men, "critics" whose rhetoric and tone, much more than their actual methods, arguments, and conclusions, demonstrate almost a moral failing or felonious intent, creating hazards for readers like her and for the field she claims to be protecting and defending.

Rather than crossing swords with any particular opponent, as noted, Felski reserves all of her postcritical criticism for a shadowy, ill-defined concept called simply "critique," which becomes queerly personified and then psychoanalyzed through a series of regrettable mixed metaphors. Consider the following passage, for example:

> Critique, it must be said, is gifted with an exceptionally talented press agent and an unparalleled mastery of public relations. Occupying the political and moral high ground in the humanities, it seems impervious to direct attack, its bulletproof vest deflecting all bursts of enemy fire. Indeed, as we'll see, even those most eager to throw a spanner into the machinery of critique—those gritting their teeth at its sheer predictability—seem powerless to bring it to a halt. The panacea they commonly prescribe, a critique of critique, might give us pause. How exactly do we quash critique by redoubling it? Shouldn't we be trying to exercise our critique-muscles less rather than more? (118)

The metaphors shift so furiously in this paragraph that the underlying argument is fairly difficult to keep up with. First, "Critique" is the name of a person who, despite being an unparalleled master of public relations, has been given a talented press agent. Critique occupies a position of such military advantage as to be impervious to attack, yet wears a bulletproof vest that repulses enemy fire; why it has enemies at all is a good question, given its well-nigh universally high approval ratings.

In the next sentence, such enemies are thwarted in advance, as Critique is now imagined as a machine whose movements are so irritatingly predictable as to cause opponents to grit their teeth, but even their spanner-throwing does nothing to slow its exorable momentum. Then this Critique person or machine quickly becomes a sort of illness or epidemic calling for a panacea, which despite the definition of the term, does not seem to cure the ailment at all. Finally, Critique is a body part belonging to all of us, like an arm or leg, whose muscles may be flexed or relaxed at will. Felski never does explain why someone with such a good press agent, "unparalleled" PR skills, and invulnerable to attack could manage to make so many enemies, but she does imagine them not only to exist but to be extraordinarily well armed themselves, while also gritting their teeth, engaging in sabotage, developing cure-alls, and flexing their own "critique-muscles." It is a rather impressive half of a paragraph, but it tells us nothing of critique other than that Felski does not like this fellow very much, wildly popular though he apparently is in her chosen field of study.

The lines quoted above appear in a chapter titled "Crrritique," literally spelled with three *R*'s, so one might assume that Felski wishes us to growl out the pronunciation of the word. I am not familiar with this convention, except in the advertisements for a brand of breakfast cereal made of frosted corn flakes, whose cartoon spokestiger assures us are "grrreat!" But then, tigers are by nature growling animals, which seems to be the point in the juxtaposition of the character with the marketing catchphrase ("They're grrreat!"). I suppose that it is possible that Felski imagines critics as growlers—we are a rather querulous bunch, as it happens—or maybe her formulation is intended to indicate the ways that postcritical scholars like herself are growling about the persistence of critique. (In fairness, Felski does not appear to be opposed to growling: "Academia has often been a haven for the disgruntled and disenchanted, for oddballs and misfits. Let us defend, without hesitation, the rights of the curmudgeonly and cantankerous!" [12].) At no point in the chapter does she explain the bizarre spelling, and apart from the title, the misspelled word appears only once, in the following, rather confusing lines:

> *Crrritique!* The word flies off the tongue like a weapon, emitting a rapid guttural burst of machine-gun-fire. There is the ominous cawing staccato of the first and final consonants, the terse thud of the short repeated vowel, the throaty underground rumble of the accompanying *r*. (120)

Leaving aside the fact that weapons do not usually fly off tongues, even metaphorically, or that the machine-gun-fire of the gut might not yield a throaty "r" sound, or that the vowel sound is not, as Felski claims, "repeated" since "crit" and "tique" (phonetically, "krih" and "tēk") hardly rhyme and do not seem to "thud," Felski's choice of spelling does seem to have value as a neologism, a unique sounding name (perhaps eligible for trademark protection?) to label this mélange of metaphors that represents the subject of her polemic or the object of her disdain. Perhaps her problem is less with critics than with *crrritics*? Yet, apart from this one instance, the more commonly spelled "critique" is used throughout *The Limits of Critique.*

One might argue that Felski is not herself antitheory, and she recognizes that theory, in some senses, is inescapable. That is, she knows well the old line about how those who claim to oppose theory are generally operating under another, often older theory. Moreover, she embraces a certain actor-network-theory (abbreviated ANT) of Bruno Latour in making her case against critique. Like the earlier form of neopragmatism, this ANT represents a somewhat antitheoretical theory, one here used to undermine the so-called high theory of such masters of suspicion as Marx, Nietzsche, Freud, and their poststructuralist, Frankfurt School, and postmodern legatees. Indeed, that sort of "theory" is sometimes labeled *critical theory*, which Felski expressly objects to on the basis of its foundational hermeneutics of suspicion. Marx and Marxism, even more than the Nietzschean and Freudian varieties of suspicion, seem to be particularly objectionable. Felski refers rather dismissively to Marx, who "sprinkles the word [*critique*] copiously through his book titles" (141); none of Marx's actual books or writings are ever cited or examined by Felski, naturally. This casual if caustic dismissal without citing any evidence is shown consistently to be the *modus operandi* of Felski's polemic.

Even with a more restrictive vision of this material as *literary theory*, Felski's position is generally anti-interpretive, favoring mere description to any attempt to generate meaning beyond surface appearances or the *status quo* as it presents itself to the reader. (The reader in this vision of things will remain mercifully untheorized as an autonomous ego, imbued with unquestioned authority, that can have an affective appreciation for the text, outside of any particular context or circumstance.) Felski's celebrated postcritical approach to literature is functionally, if not always explicitly, another attack on critical theory, and in its effects the postcritical vision is far closer to the antitheory discourse of the 1980s than is perhaps recognized. Whereas the terminology and antagonists of the old culture wars are clearly dated, the resistance to theory, antipathy toward critique, and celebration of a positive, pragmatic, and utilitarian understanding of literature is all too timely today.

Anti-Antitheory

What is to be done?...the perennial question. In the face of this assault of theory and on criticism, which now masks or simply misunderstands its ideological position with an appeal to "positive" thinking or to the defense of the humanities, I believe that a more strident and self-consciously negative critical theory is all the more needed. Indeed, I am still inclined toward the view of the young Marx, who in his famous 1843 letter to Arnold Ruge asserted that our project should entail "the ruthless critique of all that exists," and that this critique is fueled by and grounded in a profoundly critical theory.

As a purely practical matter, the argument that a more positive or even pragmatic vision of the humanities will help to save them from their enemies in state legislatures and governors' mansions and the media more broadly is, in a word, ludicrous. As Lee Konstantinou put it in the aforementioned *Chronicle of Higher Education* article, a less politicized reading of Jane Austen would not change then-Governor Scott Walker's opinion about the value of the University of Wisconsin system (quoted in Parry). The enemies of literature, of the humanities more widely, or of higher education in general are not apt to radically alter their views based on a sudden increase in the number of postcritical readings appearing in top cultural studies journals. Moreover, as Stanley Fish has warned academics tempted to win over non-academics who are skeptical of the value of literature, presenting our work in the terms of instrumental use value will either fail in principle at once or subject us to ever more rigorous measurement of "outcomes"; these new and ever more complex "metrics" will inevitably prove literary critics and scholars to be lacking in the very instrumentalized value they had claimed to offer. It is a losing strategy that has proven itself a loser for some time.

The ruthless critique of all that exists strikes me as a much better approach, and there is just so much that needs to be subjected to rigorous critique these days. Similarly, I think that the need for theory is all the greater in an epoch like ours, in which fake news, truthiness, and various visions of the "new normal" reign. To adopt a stance that is anti-antitheory also seems like a good start. This is akin to the position attributed to Sartre, who allegedly embraced the notion of "anti-anticommunism" when faced with an unacceptable Soviet-style communism on the one hand, and an almost equally abhorrent American-led anticommunism on the other. Jameson has revived the concept more recently in *Archaeologies of the Future*, where he affirms that, "for those only too wary of the motives of its critics, yet no less conscious of Utopia's structural ambiguities, those mindful of the very real political function of the idea and the program of Utopia in our time, the slogan of anti-anti-Utopianism might well offer the best working strategy" (xvi). In fact, the sort of utopian thought Jameson has in mind is of a piece with the critical theory that is still needed, since utopia was always less a blueprint of an idealized future than a satirical critique or Great Refusal, to borrow Herbert Marcuse's phrase, of the actually existing state of things. The power of the negative, something the Frankfurt School kept emphasizing throughout the twentieth century, is all the more necessary here in the United States, where even the most motivated of social critics insist upon an optimism and positive thinking that feels like a slap in the face to those facing an unjust reality, as Barbara Ehrenreich has rightly lamented.

More to my point, I think that a ruthless critique of all that exists must be undertaken from a thoroughly oppositional stance, against those who would give their support, consciously or otherwise, to an intolerable *status quo*. In terms of literary critical practice, this means continuing and expanding upon the projects that theoretically oriented criticism has made possible over the years, while making sure to subject one's own criticism to the scrutiny of a critical and theoretical perspective. In literary history, to borrow a phrase from Jonathan Arac, this is not "history from below," but "history from athwart," going against the grain to disclose or create novel connections (15). It means imagining alternatives, the very conditions for the possibility of which partly require the rejection of the tyranny of "what is." But then literature, along with literary criticism and literary theory, has always excelled at that.

For all the Black Forest gloom and prison-house austerity that the postcritical and antitheory critics perceive in the writings of Adorno, Foucault, or those who read them, there is also that unrecognized joy that comes with critique. As Jameson wrote in his introduction to *The Ideologies of Theory* (2008), "inasmuch as ideological analysis is so frequently associated with querulous and irritable negativism, it may be appropriate to stress the interest and delight all the topics, dilemmas and contradictions as well as jests and positions still have for me" (xi). Often forgotten amid the somber lessons of history, the incisive critiques of present situations, and the tenebrous forecasts of what seems likely to come is the sheer pleasure of engaging in and with critical theory. This is one more reason to be opposed to the proponents of postcritical antitheory, of course: in their insistence upon pragmatic reading, their relentlessly optative mood, and a good working relationship with the powers that be, they are trying to spoil all the fun.

Chapter 4

Reading Adorno by the Pool

Those who endorse a postcritical approach to literature, and presumably by extension a postcritical approach to other aspects of one's comportment toward the world, frequently suggest that this policy will help make literary studies, the humanities, the liberal arts, and even higher education more generally become more relevant, or perhaps "relatable," in a historical moment, social circumstance, political climate, and economic condition that seems utterly unfavorable to them. Such assertions seem misplaced, if not worse, disingenuous or dishonest, considering the circumstances in which they are made, and the notion that taking a more favorable position among the many to be found in the so-called "method wars" in literary studies would persuade pundits, politicians, or legislative bodies as to the value of literature and its need for financial support seems absurd on its face, an absurdity that the postcritical critics also recognize. Yet there remains this popular view among many in higher education that a well-publicized turn away from the "negative" aura of critique and from arcane perplexities of theory will contribute to some fantasized rescue of the humanities from the forces that oppose them. If anything, the present moment requires more critique, more theory, and indeed more critical theory.

The Polluted Sunshine of the Shopping Mall

All that is to say, maybe we need more Theodor Adorno, among others, in our lives and in our thoughts today. I suppose that the title of this chapter may seem a bit misleading at first, since my subject here is not really Adorno or his work, and it certainly does not involve swimming pools. Rather I am interested in the circumstances in which cultural criticism finds itself in our time, and I am especially concerned with the ways that major trends within criticism have abandoned theory in their pursuit of putatively empirical, pragmatic, utilitarian, or instrumental pursuits. Some of these antitheory and postcritical approaches to criticism have pointedly embraced personal affect, identification, attachment, and fandom as the core, or perhaps replacements, of literary critical engagements with texts. Other variations have taken quasi-scientific detachment and distance as the appropriate approach to literature, substituting the gathering and analysis of mere data for the meticulous analysis of particular texts, the metacommentary involved in understanding the conditions for the possibility of their interpretation, and the speculative activity necessary to situate these practices within a larger constellation of discursive practices, which are themselves part of a vaster project of making sense and give form to the world as a whole. Indeed, in their purported modesty, reverence for the texts, and greater usefulness, such methods would bring rays of sunshine into the gloom that presumably dominated the earlier heyday of literary criticism under the influence of theory.

As for the phrase itself, "reading Adorno by the pool," I borrow the image from Fredric Jameson's 1990 study of the Frankfurt School philosopher, *Late Marxism: Adorno, or, the Persistence of the Dialectic*. Those familiar with this book will recall Jameson's extraordinary thesis, which was that Adorno of all theorists, in Jameson's words,

> may turn out to have been the analyst of our own period, which he did not live to see, and in which late capitalism has all but succeeded in eliminating the final loopholes of nature and the Unconscious, of subversion and the aesthetic, of individual and collective praxis alike, and, with a final fillip, in eliminating any memory trace of what thereby no

longer existed in the henceforth postmodern landscape. (5)

Jameson, here indulging in the decade-based periodization of modern history that he had analyzed previously in "Periodizing the Sixties" (among other places), had just observed that "Adorno was surely not the philosopher of the thirties (who has to be identified in retrospect, I'm afraid, as Heidegger)," nor was he the thinker of the forties and fifties, or the sixties ("those are called Sartre and Marcuse, respectively"); and, as Jameson concedes, the seventies "were essentially French," at least in the United States. But with the arrival of the 1980s and at the threshold of the 1990s, at the advent of a postmodern condition and a post-Cold War era of globalization. At this moment, we find that "Adorno's prophecies of the 'total system' finally came true, in wholly unexpected forms." Hence, Jameson suggests—and the whole of *Late Marxism* will constitute his argument in favor of this hypothesis—that "Adorno's Marxism, which was no great help in the previous periods, may turn out to be just what we need today" (5).

Although Jameson wrote that over 30 years ago, a good case can be made to support the enduring truth of this proposition, because what might be called the "late postmodernism" of our twenty-first-century condition has, if anything, only exacerbated and extended the "total system" to which Jameson refers. The term "late postmodernism" has been used by Phillip E. Wegner, for instance, to characterize the cultural dominant of the "long Nineties" (i.e., the period between the Fall of the Berlin War in 1989 and the events of September 11, 2001), while Jeffrey Nealon has suggested "post-postmodernism" as an appropriate label for our contemporary condition, which Mark Fisher has famously recognized as one of *capitalist realism*. In the conclusion to Jameson's study, where Jameson most explicitly looks at the relationship between Adorno's critical theory and the postmodern condition, he notes that Adorno's polemics may hold the key to uncovering the theorist's special relevance, and "the persistence of the dialectic" more generally, as Jameson's subtitle would have it, in the *then*-present situation, where Adorno and Horkheimer might be able "to restore the sense of something grim and impending within the polluted sunshine of the shopping mall" (248).

Specifically, Jameson compares Adorno's critique of positivism to that era's (i.e., the 1990s') critique of postmodernism. Jameson underscores what he calls the *momentous shift* that this transcoding of positivism onto postmodernism must entail, pointing out that it would have to involve the ways that, as he puts it in his inimitable Jamesonian manner,

> a stuffy petty-bourgeois republican nineteenth-century philosophy of science emerges from the cocoon of its time capsule as the iridescent sheen of consumerist daily life in the Indian summer of the superstate and multinational capitalism. From truth to state-of-the-art merchandise, from bourgeois respectability and "distinction" to the superhighways and the beaches, from the old-fashioned authoritarian families and bearded professors to permissiveness and loss of respect for authority (which, however, still governs). (248)

Jameson concludes that paragraph with a reference to Adorno's famous (or infamous) assertion that there can be no poetry after Auschwitz: "The question about poetry after Auschwitz has been replaced with that of whether you could bear to read Adorno and Horkheimer next to the pool" (248).

Reading Adorno today may seem a bit like this, some unbearably futile attempt to counteract the dominant culture with critical theory amid a maelstrom of voices denouncing the project even as they celebrate the crises surrounding us all. True, in the 2020s culture criticism in the United States is no longer subjected to the "End of History" (in Francis Fukuyama's then-celebrated version) pundits, basking in the glow of a triumphalist, post-Cold War euphoria that characterized a lot of public discourse in the late 1980s and early 1990s. But if anything, the postmodern society of the spectacle has intensified in the twenty-first century, as has the exponential expansion of consumer capitalism, the well-nigh total media saturation of the life-world, the ideological domination of technology and engineering, the neoliberal celebrations of individualistic subjectivity as branding and entrepreneurship, and the extensions of bourgeois relations into the far reaches of the planet in connection with what was only then beginning to be called *globalization*. In such circumstances, the odd insistence that we might focus our literary studies on personal attachment, affect, and identification, as opposed to the interpretation and critique of texts, does come across as another way of saying, "Why read that dour old critical theory, when you could be enjoying the poolside comforts and sunshine?"

Resistance to Theory

On a more limited scale, perhaps, as I have been discussing, the present epoch has witnessed the widespread resurgence of largely anticritical and antitheoretical discursive practices in the humanities and social sciences. Not only has positivism itself reemerged in various forms and with greater force in the past 30 years, but also such previously vanquished old areas as ethics, pragmatism, and even metaphysics in relation to the postsecular, among other variants. Indeed, with the rise and spread of many apparently new approaches or methods in recent decades, one finds a powerful sense of political and methodological retrenchment. As a consequence, the circumstances that had made Adorno in particular, and critical theory in general, seem so old fashioned, outdated, or passé several decades ago have now developed in such a way as to call out for that good (or maybe *bad*) old-fashioned theory once again.

In a sense, I think "Adorno" can be allowed to stand as a code word for "high" theory, which I argue is precisely what is called for in the present cultural and institutional moment. If our own time is characterized in part by rampant neoliberalism, it is also very much a sort of postcritical era, inasmuch as the powers that be, along with many prominent intellectuals in the humanities, agree that the *status quo*, the surface of things, and the given (a.k.a. *data*) are to be privileged, and critique itself to be relegated to the shadows, cast as an utterly benighted and archaic practice, unsuited to and undesirable in our own time. Needless to say, perhaps, but I am in favor of enhancing the role of critical theory in a postcritical era, primarily as a means of combating it and its supporters, but this position refers less to an existing state of affairs than to a desire for alternatives: the desire for more critical theory, and specifically more theory of that older, grander variety.

As much as I want to defend what might seem to be an old-fashioned approach, I hasten to add that this is motivated not by a nostalgia for some lost Golden Age so much as by a conviction that what was so thrilling and original about the high theory of old is now somehow again timely. At the very moment when antitheoretical and postcritical approaches to literary and cultural studies have gained widespread support among prominent scholars based in prestigious institutions and publishing in celebrated journals, the need for more critique, more theory, seems all the greater. That the emergence and burgeoning of the postcritical approaches have more or less coincided with the rise of the neoliberal, corporate university and the spread of neoliberalism more generally is not surprising, as Bruce Robbins and others have observed, even if the practitioners and trumpeters of postcritique profess to be unaware of these connections.

As for our moment being discernibly "postcritical," I realize this is subject to debate. A number of major critics have already weighed in on such celebrated instances of antitheory as Rita Felski's project in *The Limits of Critique* and her ongoing work intended "to articulate a positive vision for humanistic thought in the face of growing skepticism about its value," which would apparently be accomplished by overthrowing the regnant "hermeneutics of suspicion" in contemporary literary studies and replacing it with a postcritical approach to literature (186). Throughout this book I have presented my critique of Felski's program, and there have been a number of analyses far more effective in their nuanced debunking of the postcritical project than my own, among which I would cite Robbins's "Not So Well Attached" and Anna Kornbluh's "We Have Never Been Critical" as being among the best. I would say that this postcritical and largely antitheoretical attitude associated with Felski's work also subtends a number of critical practices and "schools" that have emerged and flourished over the last several decades. Whether these are called *postcritical* or not, many of these recent methods—for example, "surface reading," "thin description," "book history," and "distant reading," along with object-oriented ontology, actor-network theory, and computational criticism, to name just a few that have been connected to what Jeffrey Williams has famously called "the new modesty" in literary criticism—implicitly or explicitly target for attack, if not simply abandon, critical theory and the interpretive practices associated with it. Indeed, one of the few things uniting such diverse movements is their general resistance to theory.

Resistance to theory, as Paul de Man and others have noted, has an illustrious history within criticism and the literary humanities, of course. De Man, in fact, notoriously argued that resistance to literary theory may well be an inherent property of theory. As he put it,

> the development of literary theory is itself overdetermined by complications inherent within its very project and unsettling

> with to its status as a scientific discipline. Resistance may be a built-in constituent of its discourse, in a manner that would be inconceivable in the natural sciences and unmentionable in the social sciences. It may well be, in other words, that the polemical opposition, the systematic non-understanding and misrepresentation, the unsubstantial but eternally recurrent objections, are the displaced symptoms of a resistance inherent to the theoretical enterprise itself. (12)

Part of the issue is summed up in the observation that "the resistance to theory is a resistance to the use of language about language" (12), and it is undoubtedly the case that one of the frustrations expressed by those who claim to oppose theory, or who feel that we would all be better off without it, is that the sense of that theory is so recursive, that it embodied a reflexivity that is then parodied as "navel gazing," and that ultimately it is thereby meaningless outside of its own practitioners' sense of self-satisfaction. This is also perhaps why so many who oppose theory seem to take their own positions so personally, and to attack those engaged in theory less on the grounds of theoretical practice *per se* and more on matters of attitude, tone, mood, stance, and style of the critical theorists themselves.

In the last few decades, a venerable procession of scholars have weighed in on the apparent abuses of critical theory. I am thinking not just of the early critiques of theory from historical or historicist thinkers such as E. P. Thompson in *The Poverty of Theory* and his fellow travelers, including even someone like Edward Said, who bemoaned the "Travelling Theory" of the late 1970s and early 1980s. The neopragmatist argument of Stephen Knapp and Walter Benn Michaels in "Against Theory" surely represents a noteworthy precursor to today's postcritical approaches, and I think it is now safe to say that, despite the dutiful and frequent name-dropping of Michel Foucault in their writings, many of the New Historicists were engaging in forms of post- or antitheoretical work as well. Indeed, the same goes for what was beginning to be labeled in a more categorical fashion "Cultural Studies" in the 1980s. In various permutations, cultural studies as a field within or adjacent to literature is now nearly ubiquitous throughout the American academe, and as Jameson had been quick to notice, it has served as a substitute for Marxism, and it has also functioned as an implicit or sometimes explicit attack on theory itself, mostly as being too abstract, too totalizing, or too bound up with grand narratives of one type or another (see "On 'Cultural Studies,'" for example). Even as its practitioners gestured toward its genealogical antecedents in Walter Benjamin's study of the Parisian arcades, the Frankfurt School's critique of the culture industry, Roland Barthes's ideological and semiotic analyses of modern myth or the fashion system, and so forth, not to mention the work of Raymond Williams, Stuart Hall, and the Birmingham School, cultural studies especially as practiced in the United States has arguably served to devalue theory and theoretical practice. Many overtly political forms of cultural and literary studies, such as feminism, queer theory, postcolonial studies, ecocriticism, and approaches attuned to matters of race or ethnic studies, have maintained their commitments to critique, especially with respect to social criticism, but they too have often abandoned "high" theory for more localized practices and pragmatism. Moreover, the digital humanities and other more technology-oriented fields that have developed in recent years have their own theories and uses of theory, but generally in the service of antitheoretical programs. (In some cases, rather complex and innovated theory has been put to good use in criticizing the work in these fields, as with Alexander Galloway's timely interventions.) Of course, in all of these disparate approaches, there are those who remain engaged with literary and critical theory to a greater or lesser degree, but as a whole, these various "schools" may be characterized by their resistance to, and sometimes their rejection of, theory.

The Consequences of Distant Reading

Another twenty-first-century approach is worth discussing, since it was largely developed by and championed by a critic who has been throughout his career generally pro-theory, quite critical, and Marxist to boot. I refer to the "distant reading" project of Franco Moretti, which he pursued with zeal for the last 2 decades until his recent retirement. Moretti had announced his project in two influential essays published almost simultaneously in 2000, "Conjectures on World Literature" and "The Slaughterhouse of Literature," where he introduced the term—a playful twist on New Critical, deconstructive, or otherwise formalist versions of "close reading"—in connection with a new project that would involve "other skills: sampling; statistics; work with series, titles, concordances, incipits," thereby producing a literary history that would "become 'second hand': a patchwork of other people's research, *without a single direct textual reading*" (*Distant Reading*, 67, 48). Adopting new technologies to accompany this new methodology, Moretti thus goes beyond the critics who had opposed a hermeneutics of suspicion or the "against interpretation" position (Susan Sontag, e.g.); even "surface reading" is far too interpretative a practice to one who favors "distant reading."

In *Graphs, Maps, Trees: Abstract Models for a Literary History* (2005), Moretti proposes these three "tools" that could be used for the sorts of distant reading projects he imagines, whereby—once the data can be visually diagrammed using a map, a graph, or a tree—the models themselves would be subject to a kind of interpretation or data analysis, but again, no specific novels would ever be read by the "distant reader." The publication in 2013 of *Distant Reading,* which collects "Conjectures," "Slaughterhouse," and many other of his key essays on the subject, and of *The Bourgeois: Between History and Literature,* a study produced in large part via the distant reading method, revealed the extent to which Moretti's new science of literary history, one which eschewed reading entirely in favor of "data," could operate in Moretti's own readings. As he had said, this sort of work would involve a great deal of collaborative effort, and *Canon/Archive* (2017), a collection of published studies conducted by his Literary Lab at Stanford, appears to mark the culmination and the end of Moretti's direct engagement with what he had also referred to as "the computational analysis of literature" (*Distant Reading* 211). Although it was much celebrated at the time, it is not clear how influential distant reading itself remains, but the approach to literary studies that Moretti was modeling and its rejection, tacit or otherwise, of critical theory has had pervasive consequences.

When Moretti introduced the idea of distant reading in his 2000 essay "Conjectures on World Literature," he did so in part to deal with a problem he posed in its companion-piece, "The Slaughterhouse of Literature": namely, how can a critic ever really discuss "world literature" or even more limited national literatures, given the fact that the field of literature includes far more texts that anyone could ever possibly read? Considering that all literary critics and historians were thus limiting their study to a tiny fraction of the literature actually published, Moretti argued that other means would be required to assess the field as a whole. Moretti's idea of "distant reading" is intended as a provocation, aimed at proponents of textual analysis from William K. Wimsatt to Jacques Derrida; that is, "the very close reading of very few texts," a practice that in Moretti's somewhat snarky view has radiated from the cheerful town of New Haven over the whole field of literary studies, would have to be abandoned, as would any theory of language or literature tied to such a critical activity. Distant reading, by contrast, would offer a new way of seeing literature which was made possible by looking at data rather than texts themselves.

Moretti's project did not merely require an innovative style of interpreting texts, but a wholesale abandonment of interpretative practice in favor of other methods. It will involve a new sort of "surface reading," although here the surface is not that of the text itself—the mere reading of the words on a page—but the multivalent superficies produced by a variety of forms of survey, mostly involving databases and scanning through troves of information in different electronic ensembles. Distant reading requires quantitative analysis, and since it must also rely upon data gathered by others, "second hand," as Moretti put it, distant reading will also embrace the possibilities of or need for collaborative research. As he says in *Graphs, Maps, Trees*, "quantitative work is truly *cooperative*: not only in the pragmatic sense that it takes forever to gather the data, but because such data are ideally independent from any individual researcher, and can thus be shared by others, and combined in more than one way" (5). The gathering, organizing, and analyzing of data would be essential. Instead of looking at the words, phrases, sentences, or other formal features of individual stories, novels, poems, plays, or other texts, the distant reader will examine other units, "much smaller or much larger than the text: devices, themes, tropes—or genres and systems" (*Distant Reading* 48–49). Hence, distant reading is not imagined as a supplementary approach to close reading; rather, it involves an entirely new sense of literary critical and literary historical practice, one in which texts are no longer read at all, in which interpretation of literature yields to data collection and data analysis.

"Big Data," as it came to be called in the early twenty-first-century, was in many ways both the prerequisite for and the *modus operandi* of this new form of antitheoretical and postcritical "distant reading." As an aside, perhaps, a materialist historian might observe in passing that this project coincided with Moretti's move from the rather bookish Ivy League redoubt of Columbia University to Silicon Valley's own ivory tower at Stanford, where utopian visions of "big data" and its socially transformative potential were all the rage in the early 2000s.

Such proximity is not dispositive of anything, but one does wonder what effects, if any, the neoliberal *Zeitgeist* (and even the *Raumgeist*) may have had on the formerly Marxist critic's views of literary analysis and ideology critique.

In 2017, as part of a special section of *PMLA* devoted to his *Distant Reading*, Moretti offered his own retrospective assessment of the work that he and his team in the Stanford Literary Lab had undertaken. He candidly admitted that the project was mostly a failure, conceding that his aspirations in dabbling with these dark arts were not realized. Moretti was nevertheless unapologetic, saying (as quoted in a contemporaneous *New York Times* article) "I'd rather be a failed revolutionary…than someone who never tried to do a revolution in the first place" (see Schuessler, "Reading by the Numbers: When Big Data Meets Literature"). However, he also identified an area in which his own work has been adversely affected by his decision to engage in "computational criticism," as he there referred to it. Moretti admitted that his research had suffered from a *lack of theory*, and, in an understated aside, he confessed, "to be frank, I think it's true of the digital humanities as a whole." A certain glibness takes over in these practices, Moretti observed, and knowledge itself winds up being the victim. He confessed in his "Response" to the *PMLA*'s essays on *Distant Reading* that,

> Time after time, I have felt myself (and others?) slip into microexplanations; ad hoc, often improvised reactions to the pressure of this or that finding, which I couldn't connect with any broader horizon. Knowledge seemed to shrink into half-knowledge; a false modesty, bordering on intellectual hide-and-seek; or the coarse anti-intellectualism exemplified by *Wired*'s proclamation that "correlation is enough" and that "the scientific method" is "obsolete." (687)

(Moretti's reference to *Wired* magazine's glib dismissal of the scientific method is all the more noteworthy at a time when skeptics of the putative "fake news" abound and a global pandemic rages unabated.) Moretti's project, perhaps unwittingly, perhaps not, contributed to this anti-critical and antitheoretical tendency in contemporary literary studies, and Moretti is wise enough to know that was a problem. "Fact is," Moretti notes, "big data has produced a decline in theoretical interest, which, it its turn, has made our results often mediocre. 'More' data is not the solution here; we have enough data already. Only a resolute return to theory may change the way we work" (687).

I agree, and I want to argue that a "resolute return to theory" is precisely what is needed for literary and cultural criticism today. This would entail a return to forms of close reading, if only to acknowledge the degree to which the details and minutiae are absolutely constitutive of the broader issues to be grasped at a "big picture" level. The creative and speculative aspects of critical theory have always been part and parcel of a meticulously interpretative practice attuned to the complex interrelations among the parts and the whole. Ironically, perhaps, it may be that the critical distance afforded by a return to theorizing could take advantage of the resources made available by computers and databases without succumbing to the Silicon Valley's mania for technology-enabled "disruption," just as literary studies need not shed its connections to critical theory in pursuit of popular approval or official governmental or corporate sanction. Critique remains the most effective form by which to understand those texts under consideration—*texts* broadly conceived so as to include their contexts and conditions of possibility, as well as their resonances with and implications for meaningful considerations of other texts—and to reveal their potential to open up new vistas and vantages, giving imaginative shape to both the world we live in and to radical alternatives to it. Critical theory is thus an essential element of literature in an age of capitalist realism.

Untimely Theory

Advocates for a sort of antitheory and postcritique, as these manifest themselves in contemporary literary critical practice, thus wind up capitulating to a neoliberal ideology and social system, even as they themselves may be radically opposed to the specific political policies associated with them. The turn away from speculative thinking, from metacommentary, and from interpretation becomes a turn toward accepting the *status quo* as is, toward taking it as a natural state of affairs, and toward assuming that what we see is all that can possibly exist. Without theory, as Moretti suggested in retrospect, literary criticism is far too reliant on, and is mostly limiting itself to, the merely "given," that is, *data,* whereas the fundamental bailiwick of literature lies precisely beyond the given, in the multifaceted, protean, and ever-expanding territories of the imagination.

It is not merely the antitheory crowd. Amid the variously antitheoretical or postcritical strains of literary critical discourses in recent decades, there have also been many who defended theory and maintained a pro-theory attitude. These tend to fall into one of two camps: on the one hand, those who mourn the death of theory, following such critics as Terry Eagleton (in *After Theory*) in eulogizing the great works and figures of the past, but who hold out little hope for the prospects of theory today; and, on the other hand, those who see in our era's widespread multiplication of critical movements and techniques a "theory renaissance," to cite Vincent Leitch's optimistic slogan from his study *Literary Criticism in the 21st Century*. The former are apt to feel nostalgic for the epoch of "high theory," when poststructuralism, semiotics, feminism, psychoanalysis, and Western Marxism jostled each other for critical dominance in literary and cultural studies, with the frequent result of creating revolutionary new ways of experiencing the world and our engagements with it. (Some of the former, alternatively, might also mourn what they take to be the ossification of theory into various types of dogmatic thinking, professional jargon, or institutionalized "best practices," none of which makes room for the imaginative possibilities associated with "*Theory*-with-a-capital-T" in its prime.) Whereas the latter might find in the dissipation and diffusion of earlier theory across disciplinary fields and into new areas of inquiry a more vibrant, diverse critical ecosystem, in which a wide variety of critical practices thrive alongside one another in ways that may not necessarily transform our world, but that productively illuminate its features. For example, Leitch identifies "94 subdisciplines and fields circling around 12 major topics" (vi), which are necessarily minor, limited, and technical compared with the grand theoretical traditions of yore. In that view, the delights of theory are available to all, much as a well-stocked supermarket can offer dozens of versions of the products we seek, some far more attractive than others (given our own tastes, among other considerations), but all equally valid choices in the vast marketplace of literary critical ideas. To be sure, there is no shortage of "theory" to be found even in an era when prominent critics embrace postcritical and antitheory positions. Regarding the nostalgic mourners of theory's lost grandeur and the more sanguine supporters of what they take to be a proliferation of theoretical practices, one could say that both perspectives have value, but neither is particularly helpful for dealing with our present condition.

Instead of looking back elegiacally at some memorable but no longer accessible Golden Age of theory and instead of taking an optimistic view of the evermore various practices emerging and sometimes predominating literary studies at present, I think we should try to return, in admittedly altered circumstances, to those aspects of high theory that most effectively speak to our present condition. There is no question that the theorists of the past were grappling with the intellectual and social crises of their own times, and that therefore their work ought to be understood in its historical context. However, it is also true that theory, like literature, often speaks to us in our own moment and our own condition, sometimes with profoundly transformative effects both on the theories in question and on ourselves.

Nietzsche's vision of the *unzeitgemässe* or "untimely" thought serves as a model of that which resists the dichotomy of crudely historicized and thus unnecessarily circumscribed thinking of a given moment and the unacceptably vague or diffuse idea of some transhistorical (or ahistorical), universal ideas. Perhaps we may seek out that which was *untimely* in what some would consider "old-fashioned" theory, and find it well suited to our own times. Or, to cite another prominent literary critical, we might draw upon Raymond Williams's helpful distinction between *emergent*, *dominant*, and *residual* forms from his *Marxism and Literature*, insofar as we can seek what was truly emergent in those older theories, and we may find them now to be thoroughly appropriate to the cultural dominant of the present.

This is part of what Jameson had in mind in proposing Adorno as the philosopher for the post-1989 moment, an era of post-Cold War ideological and consumerist triumphalism in the United States. The heady delirium of the "End of History" moment of the early 1990s, which was itself a time of social crisis and widespread *angst* even within the supposedly victorious "West," has since given way to greater cultural anxieties and sociopolitical conundrums, such that this period of economic recession, plus "grunge rock" and "reality bites," amid other Gen X *whatever*...all this somehow seems like the halcyon days of yore for today's over-parented, debt-ridden, and widely maligned Millennials and utterly despondent and thus brilliantly cynical Gen Z adversaries who mercifully take up arms against each other or else the Baby Boomers in popular culture and social media now. The generational warfare, in a manner somewhat similar to the ways in which different forms of identity politics have carved out divisions within the exploited and the exploiters, provides both a veil and a movie-screen, an entertaining backdrop for the playing out of superficial antagonisms while the real powers within late capitalist societies infused with neoliberal politics continue their business as usual while also enjoying the show. I suspect that the once celebrated analysis of the "culture industry" by Adorno and Horkheimer from the 1940s is, in fact, all the more relevant today, perhaps even more so than in its own moment.

A Joyous Counter-Poison

Within academe, the attacks on critical theory within literary studies have become increasingly forceful and nuanced since the late 1980s, which not coincidentally coincides with the most vocal, vicious, and politically effective attacks on higher education, on the humanities, and on literature as a field. Perversely, perhaps, one apparent motivation behind these arguments for surface reading and postcritical approaches is the desire to "sell" the humanities to the public. For example, Felski has argued that "critique" itself has alienated literature professors from the broader public, and that the postcritical approach to literature will reconnect scholars with the public at large. She asserts that the "vision" that motivates her desire for a postcritical approach to literature is "sorely needed if we are to make a more compelling case for why the arts and humanities are needed" (186). Of course, as a literature professor and critic myself, I am extremely sympathetic to this vision and to its motives, but I have many reservations with respect to its methods and effects. As Stanley Fish—of all people!—has observed, "marketing" literary studies to those who do not value literature will inevitably serve the interests of our opponents and undermine the field further. Fish is arguing that literature operates outside the purview of those instrumental or political aims that sometimes infect our defenses of the field, as a means of instilling critical thinking skills useful for the workplaces of the future or of making students more empathetic and better-informed citizens ready to meet the social challenges of an era of globalization or whatever. A postcritical vision of literary studies in terms of personal affect, attachment, and appreciation seems like a particularly cheery version of these otherwise instrumentalist justifications for literature.

In the sort of vision animating the surface reading, postcritical, antitheoretical approach to literary studies, studying and teaching literature are expressly reimagined as a product for public consumption, and this seems to me to be part of its problem. By appealing to the mass market, it must bask in what Jameson called "the polluted sunshine of the shopping mall," ignoring or blind to what all this entails. For one thing, arguably, it compromises the very position of the literary critic or professor entirely, by championing an approach to literature that removes scholarly expertise and even more general knowledge from the process. Why should one study literature with a learned expert when one can simply ascertain, or actually "feel," all that is worthwhile from a given text by reading its surface, something that anyone, regardless of experience or guidance, can do on one's own? And why should universities employ experts to teach these works, once it becomes clear that readers will learn all they need to know by experiencing the texts unmediated by theory or method? Non-specialists could certainly provide the reading lists for such work; so could representatives from textbook publishers, or those in marketing departments of other corporations. In fact, it seems more likely that a corporate marketing version of literature would emerge from a postcritical and antitheoretical literature curriculum than a sudden efflorescence of public funding of and popular acclaim for the humanities in colleges and universities.

A postcritical approach that encourages readers to trust their own affective reaction to whatever "brand" of literature seems most commercially attractive to them at any given moment certainly does serve the interests of neoliberalism, both at the more abstract ideological level and right down to consumer habits and commodity purchases. Within the university, moreover, such a theory of literature comports well with institutional practices of increased adjunctification and precarity, since the "surface reading" can be accomplished as easily by non-experts as by professionally trained scholars. Indeed, adjunct faculty members are already and will likely continue to be professionally trained scholars and experts, but the point is that adherents of this philosophy of literature and of its pedagogy do not care whether the instructor is knowledgeable. As I say, what would prevent neoliberal universities from outsourcing all teaching to the textbook manufacturers or marketers, who could easily supply their own representatives to "teach" literature in this manner, other than current accreditation standards? (It is disturbing to see prominent literature professors advocating practices that would effectively lower such standards.) The seemingly sunny disposition of critics like Felski, who oppose the ostensibly "negative" attitudes of those "suspicious minds" influenced by a baleful "hermeneutics of suspicion," may seem all the more ironic, considering the dire consequences of these ideas.

I would argue that a less commodified, more overtly critical literary theory and practice can disclose the cleansing gloom that is opposed to this false light. As Jameson put it, "nothing truly interesting is possible without negativity" ("On 'Cultural Studies'" 633). Such negations may be all the more welcome amid the forced smiles and odiously upbeat attitudes of the defenders of the *status quo* these days. In referring to Adorno's notoriously dour disposition, which undoubtedly makes it all the more difficult to read *Dialectic of Enlightenment* or other works while sitting beside the pool, Jameson points out that, happily, Adorno's "bile is a joyous counter-poison and a corrosive solvent to apply to the surface of 'what is'" (*Late Marxism* 249). Given that "what is" is profoundly intolerable to so many people today, this "bile" must be all the more welcome.

Concluding on a slightly more positive, though not positivist, note, I would offer the following, drawing upon a marvelous metaphor from Ernst Bloch. If we imagine that the critical theory of the past is somehow no longer as effective or valuable for us today, we may still look upon such grand theory as so much "gold-bearing rubble." The "high theory" found in the work of such thinkers as Benjamin, Lukács, Adorno, Sartre, Fanon, Lacan, Kristeva, Foucault, Deleuze, or Jameson (to name but a few), having been worked, reworked, modified, abandoned, and recovered, now speaks to the present critical condition in fresh ways. Again, this is not to dismiss the historical specificity of the theorists or theories in question, but to highlight the manner in which such theory proleptically illuminates and complicates the vital questions we face in the twenty-first century. Sifting through the rubble of what had been left of "Theory-with-a-capital 'T,'" we can reaffirm the power of critical and speculative practice, what Bloch called "the lastingly subversive and utopian contents" of such theory (116), for literary and cultural criticism today.

Conclusion

Recipes for the Cook-Shops of the Future

Almost exactly 40 years after Karl Marx had asserted that "we have no business with the construction of the future or with organizing it for all time" and called for "a ruthless critique of all that exists" as the only, but still most urgent, task facing revolutionaries at the time, Marx revisited the theme in the Afterword to the second edition of *Capital*, a work that perhaps stands as one of the greatest "critiques" of all time. Responding to a comment in a French review, published in the Paris-based *Revue Positiviste*—a journal founded by followers of Auguste Comte, and hence one that promoted the sort of positivism that Marx, and later Theodor Adorno, Michel Foucault, Fredric Jameson, and other critical theorists more generally would criticize—Marx scoffs at the objection that he was "confining myself merely to the critical analysis of the actual facts, instead of writing recipes (Comtist ones?) for the cook-shops of the future" (*Capital* 99). Marx thus simultaneously rejects the temptation to turn Marxism into a form of futurology, and he reaffirms its commitment to critical analysis.

The line about "recipes for cook-shops of the future" has often been cited as a justification for not producing blueprints of future communist or otherwise utopian societies. And it is true that a basic tenet of historical materialism would hold that we who are *situated* in a given time and place are not privy to the details of what an entirely different social formation would look like. Marx's own strenuous critiques of "utopian socialists," in *The Communist Manifesto* and elsewhere, along with Engels's later *Socialism: Utopian and Scientific*, serve to disavow calls for such blueprint-utopias. However, as Jameson especially has made clear throughout his career, a powerfully utopian impulse lies at the heart of the project of Marxist criticism. Indeed, drawing upon what Jameson has referred to as "the dialectic of utopia and ideology" in *The Political Unconscious*, we could say that critique itself embodies elements of this utopianism.

Fundamentally, as I have been arguing in this book, critique serves to educate and empower the imagination, and I would call attention to the "recipe" (*Rezepte*) part of Marx's famous phrase, rather than the "future," as what he is really objecting to. That is, as Marx had already suggested in 1843 in his letter to Arnold Ruge and as he maintained in this 1873 Afterword, the proper response to questions about any imagined *future* will have to involve a ruthless critique of all that exists *in the present*. The future is not thereby ignored; in fact, it is absolutely crucial to the overall project. Critique is essentially an act of the imagination.

Opponents of "critique" in literary studies over the past 20 years or so have often complained about the moral tone or attitude of what they take to be the paranoid, suspicious, or symptomatic readers engaged in critique. Eve Kosofsky Sedgwick's references to the "paranoid reader" as "cruel," "contemptuous," and "ugly" (144) are striking, so much so that David Kurnick has observed that "it is difficult to separate this argument about hermeneutic method from a characterology, even a demonology" (364). Many of the critics of paranoid, symptomatic, or suspicious modes of engaging in literary criticism wish to emphasize that those interpretive practices are not only untrustworthy or somehow morally objectionable. Sometimes their immorality is even cast as an aspect of the method itself, with an additional *ad hominem* attack implied, as when critique-minded readers are depicted as unfairly "looking down" on the texts in question, their authors, "mere" readers, or other interpretations. Depictions of the critic as elitist, arrogant, domineering, pedantic, and cynical are not uncommon, as we have seen.

And yet this moralizing characterization and critique of *critique* could not be farther from the spirit of proper critique, particularly in its Marxist variants. Jameson, for example, has long insisted that the very nature of dialectical thought militates against such moralizing, since the changing historical situation may prove one's previously moral stance to have been retroactively made to appear immoral. In *Marxism and Form,* Jameson writes that

> [t]he basic story the dialectic has to tell is no doubt that of the dialectical *reversal,* that paradoxical turning around of a phenomenon into its opposite of which the transformation of quality into quantity is only one of the better known manifestations. It can be described as a kind of leap-frogging affair in time, in which the drawbacks of a given historical situation turn out in reality to have been its secret advantages, in which what looked like built-in superiorities suddenly prove to be the most ironclad limits on its future development. It is a matter, indeed, of the reversal of limits, of the transformation from negative to positive and from positive to negative; and is basically a diachronic process. (309)

Almost 40 years later, he reaffirmed this in *Valences of the Dialectic,* where he also shows how moralizing is anathematic to dialectical criticism: "[t]he dialectic is an injunction to think the negative and the positive together at one and the same time, in the unity of a single thought, there where moralizing wants to have the luxury of condemning this evil without particularly imagining anything else in its place" (421). Jameson adds that this "ambivalence" is necessary, inasmuch as "what is currently negative can also be imagined as positive in that immense changing of the valences which is the Utopian future" (423). A given critique may be motivated by moral convictions, but it cannot operate properly if it succumbs to any type of moralizing thought.

Phillip E. Wegner, in his *Invoking Hope: Theory and Utopia in Dark Times*, takes up this issue in advocating for a vision of critique as a combination of *generous thinking*, *deep listening*, and *creative reading*, which combine into a commitment to theory and utopia in our teaching, our writing, and our lives. These are the elements Wegner locates in *critical theory*, which like utopian thought has come under increasingly persistent attack both within and outside the humanities in recent decades, effectively reinforcing the attitude of capitalism realism. Much of the power of *Invoking Hope* lies in how seamlessly it is able to present *theory* and *utopia* as necessarily correlates, and how this theory is part of the creative, generous, and critical practices from which the features of any utopia are made cognizable. "Learning any theory is akin to learning a new language," Wegner writes, "and hence theory is the very possibility of reading, writing, and thinking the world" (19).

These practices are nicely tied together in Wegner's notion of creative reading, which connects the various conceptual threads spun forth in *Invoking Hope* and which itself models the sort of method that I understand as critique, in contrast to the ridiculous stereotypes conjured up by postcritical opponents of symptomatic reading. In particular, the theory and practice of creative reading enacts the generosity and patience so necessary to move beyond the merely polemical into a more constructive practice related to it. Needless to say, perhaps, I do still think there is plenty of room for polemic, so long as we do not allow ourselves to become smitten with it and to thus ignore its necessary follow-up work: namely, to discover and make knowable those aspects of the utopian prospect in whatever may at this moment and in the present configuration seem utterly dark or hopeless. Like Jameson, who is the exemplar of this sort of creative reader, Wegner insists that any critique of the present is incomplete if it does not also identify some potential, incipient, or emergent forms of radical alternatives. Our inability to see those forms may say less about the texts in question, including the social texts that constitute our present sense of reality, than it does about our own ways of reading. By failing to deliver possible alternatives or to inspire our imaginations beyond this or that sort of consumerist self-regard, surface reading and postcritique may wind up sparking our imaginations despite themselves, if only because our imaginations will grow restless under the strains of the limits imposed by superficial reading.

Along these lines, Anna Kornbluh offers a powerful defense of the value of critical theory as a fundamentally constructive activity in her recent study *The Order of Forms: Realism, Formalism, and Social Space*. There she argues for a "political formalism" that would overcome aspects of the seesaw debates within literary studies over the priority of formalism or historicism, much as Jameson himself had done in *The Political Unconscious*. Kornbluh rejects the postcritical approaches even as she questions other deconstructive practices as well, and she explicitly argues for a robust form of Marxist critical reading and theory that would help both to make clearer sense of the world and to build alternative, more desirable forms. Given the profound, complex issues facing us in our social lives in the twenty-first century, one might ask—as skeptics often do when facing innovative interpretations of texts or theories in literary or cultural studies—what critical readings of nineteenth-century novels have to do with our political struggles in the "real world." But Kornbluh magisterially connects the social and political program she envisions to a formalist approach to literature, noting that

> [t]he study of literary form is at root the analysis of how language furnishes a medium for composing sustained repetitions, delimited contours, performative conjurings,

> and synthetic abstractions. Experts in these constructions are equipped, I contend, to understand and even engineer parallel formations in the phenomenal realm of everyday life, in everyday space in everyday institutions, as these too emerge in the medium of language. (4–5)

As Kornbluh observes, such attention to and valuation of form in literary studies, particularly in recognizing the ways that realism projects forms that are essential for living, makes possible the political project of form-building in our world today. This argument brings architecture (i.e., the modeling of social space) and mathematics (the modeling of possible space) to bear on realism, which Kornbluh deftly redefines as a "speculative projection of hypothetical social space, where 'social space' signals the medium of collective life" (30). In other words, realism does not so much reflect existing social forms as it actively shapes them.

Kornbluh's inspirational recasting of the project of realism, along with that of literary criticism and theory, as simultaneously analytical and constructive goes a long way toward radically transforming the concept of *capitalist realism* as well. Whereas Mark Fisher had coined the term as a way of registering contemporary culture's inability to imagine alternatives to the current socioeconomic and political order of things, Kornbluh suggests ways that realism itself can open up new spaces of imaginative possibilities, along with models of collective, political form-building for a future that can be entirely distinct from the world we know. In some respects, this is very much like Herbert Marcuse's "scandal of qualitative difference," which was itself another way of imagining utopian thought and collective action at once.

Critics must play their role in helping to empower the imagination that in turn will make these new forms possible. Academics do this in the classroom all the time—as Jameson has asserted, "Pedagogy is not inflicting discipline but awakening interest" ("Revisiting" 151)—but this critical attitude, Foucault's "art of voluntary insubordination" and Marx's "ruthless critique of all that exists," must remain an essential element of our research, writing, and thinking as well. To quote that old Kantian slogan, *Sapere aude!*, we must dare to be wise, which in turn must now also mean that we must dare to imagine radical alternatives to the present condition, which itself has become increasingly intolerable.

In an interview from April 2020, Jürgen Habermas—that grand legatee of both the Kantian and Marxist forms of critique, along with the Frankfurt School of Social Research's critical theory—reflected on the current state of affairs, and although he was responding in particular to questions raised by the coronavirus crisis, his comments extended to a more general condition of life in the twenty-first century. "One thing can be said," Habermas concluded, "There has never been as much knowledge about our ignorance and about the compulsion to act and to live with uncertainty" (*Eines kann man sagen: So viel Wissen über unser Nichtwissen und über den Zwang, unter Unsicherheit handeln und leben zu müssen, gab es noch nie*). Jokes about "known unknowns" aside, it is true that our present situation is charactered by a profound sense of uncertainty, and that the existential condition (i.e., one characterized by *angst*, above all) in the face of that uncertainty is perhaps greater than ever before. We *know* that we *don't know*, which is far more disconcerting than merely *not knowing*. At this precarious moment in world history, merely making sense of the present itself must require robust critical theory and interpretive practices, for no matter what the "just reading" or "surface reading" advocates argue, we cannot *know* for sure what is happening as we navigate the scene and imagine a future.

Citing Habermas's comments, Slavoj Žižek emphasizes this point. Any plans for the future, which must inevitably also be ways of acting and living in the present, must take into account our profound knowledge of our ignorance, our *Wissen über unser Nichtwissen*. As Žižek explains,

> [w]hen we try to guess how our societies will look after the pandemic will be over, the trap to avoid is futurology—futurology by definition ignores our not-knowing. Futurology is defined as a systematic forecasting of the future from the present trends in society. And therein resides the problem—futurology mostly extrapolates what will come from the present tendencies. However, what futurology doesn't take into account are historical "miracles," radical breaks which can only be explained retroactively, once they happen.

As Žižek sums up in the end, "Futurology deals with what is possible, we need to do what is (from the standpoint of the existing global order) impossible."

Here "radical break" becomes another code word for utopia, as Jameson might say, and as he has said, in *Archaeologies of the Future*. There he also observed that, perhaps, "we need to develop an anxiety about losing the future which is analogous to Orwell's anxiety about the loss of the past and of memory" (233). In our collective moment of neoliberal political policies, capitalist exploitation on a truly global scale, pervasive economic uncertainty, widespread social unrest, a worldwide pandemic, and the looming specter and insistent reality of climate change, this anxiety may already be all too well instilled within us. This makes our time particularly well suited to a ruthless critique of all that exists, a critique that also holds true to the wonderfully imaginative political slogan of what seems a more optimistic epoch, *Be realistic: Demand the impossible!*

David McNally has written that "critical theory sets out to see the unseen, to chart the cartography of the invisible" (6). This figure aptly represents the sort of *Ideologiekritik* that would lift the veil of a perniciously false appearance to reveal the hidden reality beneath it, but it also calls to mind that utopian dimension in which we may attempt to imagine the future, which is surely the most significant "unseen" reality there is. The same Marx who called for a ruthless critique of all that exists, while anticipating the objections of those anti-critical forces of his day (and ours), observed that "[c]ritique has torn the imaginary flowers from the chain not in order that man shall continue to bear that chain without fantasy or consolation, but so that he shall throw off the chain and pluck the living flower" (*Early Writings* 244). As Marx and Engels would put it a few years later while encouraging working people of the world to unite, ultimately we have nothing to lose but these chains, but we also have the world to win.

The essence of critique, contrary to its calumnious characterization as a "negative" or "arrogant" practice, is in fact a kind of *fröhlich Wissenschaft*, a gay science imbued with joyful wisdom, to cite another "master of suspicion," Friedrich Nietzsche. Critique, like the creative reading and speculative theorizing it requires, is a utopian practice as well. Critique provides much needed illumination, dispersing the darkness and bringing to light those figures of radical alterity legible to those who can but see them; it can also temper and provide shade from the baleful spotlight, so brilliant and dazzling, relentlessly shone upon us in a neoliberal system of capitalist realism. Literature has always served to give shape to both the dark and the light spaces of our world, and literary criticism and theory can do its part to help us make sense of those shapes and to discern different ones. These would not be recipes for the cook-shops of the future—what future shops would want our recipes, after all?—but would enable us to better read, write, and think this world of ours, and also to imagine alternatives.

Bibliography

Anker, Elizabeth S., and Rita Felski, eds. *Critique and Postcritique*. Durham: Duke University Press, 2017.

Arac, Jonathan. "Nationalism, Hypercanonization, and *Huckleberry Finn*." *boundary* 2 19.1 (Spring 1992), 14–33.

Barry, Peter. *Beginning Theory: An Introduction to Literary and Cultural Theory*. 3rd ed. Manchester: Manchester University Press, 2009.

Bartolovich, Crystal. "Humanities of Scale: Marxism, Surface Reading—and Milton." *PMLA* 127, no. 1 (2013): 115–121.

Bauerlein, Mark. "Where are the Literary Scholars/Theorists?" *Chronicle of Higher Education* online (April 26, 2010): http://www.chronicle.com/blogs/brainstorm/where-are-the-literary-scholars-theorists/23481.

Best, Stephen, and Sharon Marcus. 2009. "Surface Reading: An Introduction." *Representations* 108: 1–21.

Bloch, Ernst. *Heritage of Our Times*. Trans. Neville and Stephen Plaice. Berkeley: University of California Press, 1991.

Bové, Paul A. *In the Wake of Theory*. Hanover, N.H.: Wesleyan University Press, 1992.

—. *Love's Shadow*. Cambridge: Harvard University Press, 2021.

Canavan, Gerry. 2019. "Disney's Endgame: How the Franchise Came to Rule Cinema." *Frieze* (December 6, 2019): https://frieze.com/article/disneys-endgame-how-franchise-came-rule-cinema.

Chibber, Vivek. "Orientalism and Its Afterlives." *Catalyst* 4.3 (2020): https://catalyst-journal.com/vol4/no3/orientalism-and-its-afterlives.

Cole, Andrew. *The Birth of Theory*. Chicago: University of Chicago Press, 2014.

Crews, Frederick. *The Pooh Perplex*. Chicago: University of Chicago Press, 2003.

—. *Postmodern Pooh*. New York: North Point Press, 2001.

de Man, Paul. *The Resistance to Theory*. Minneapolis: University of Minnesota Press, 1986.

Di Leo, Jeffrey R., ed. *What's Wrong with Antitheory?* New York: Bloomsbury, 2019.

Eagleton, Terry. *After Theory*. Cambridge, MA: Basic Books, 2004.

—. *Literary Theory: An Introduction*. Minneapolis: University of Minnesota Press, 1983.

Edwards, Caroline. "Uncovering the 'gold-bearing rubble': Ernst Bloch's Literary Criticism." In *Utopianism, Modernism, and Literature in the Twentieth Century*, eds. Alice Reeve-Tucker and Nathan Waddell. Basingstoke: Palgrave Macmillan, 2013. 182–203.

Ehrenreich, Barbara. *Bright-Sided: How Positive Thinking is Undermining America*. New York: Metropolitan Books, 2010.

Felski, Rita. *Hooked: Art and Attachment*. Chicago: University of Chicago Press, 2020.

—. *The Limits of Critique*. Chicago: University of Chicago Press, 2015.

—. "My Sociology Envy." *Theory, Culture, and Society* blog (July 25, 2019): https://www.theoryculturesociety.org/blog/think-pieces-rita-felski-my-sociology-envy.

—. *Uses of Literature*. Oxford: Blackwell, 2008.

Fish, Stanley. "Always Academicize." *The New York Times*, opinion online (Nov. 5, 2006): https://opinionator.blogs.nytimes.com/2006/11/05/always-academicize-my-response-to-the-responses/.

—. *Is There a Text in This Class?* Cambridge: Harvard University Press, 1980.

Foucault, Michel. "What is Critique?" Trans. Lysa Hochroth. In *The Politics of Truth*, eds. Sylvère Lotringer. New York: Semiotext(e), 1997. 41–81.

Grattan, Sean. *Hope Isn't Stupid: Utopian Affects in Contemporary*

American Literature. Iowa City: University of Iowa Press, 2017.

Habermas, Jürgen. "Jürgen Habermas über Corona." Interview with Markus Schwering. *Frankfurter Rundschau* (April 10, 2020): https://www.fr.de/kultur/gesellschaft/juergen-habermas-coronavirus-krise-covid19-interview-13642491.html.

Harvey, David. *A Brief History of Neoliberalism*. Oxford: Oxford University Press, 2007.

Huehls, Mitchum. *After Critique: Twenty-First-Century Fiction in a Neoliberal Age*. Oxford: Oxford University Press, 2016.

Jameson, Fredric. *Allegory and Ideology*. London: Verso, 2019.

—. *Archaeologies of the Future: The Desire Called Utopia and Other Science Fictions*. London: Verso, 2005.

—. "Future City." *The Ideologies of Theory*. London: Verso, 2008. 563–576.

—. *The Ideologies of Theory*. London: Verso, 2008.

—. *Late Marxism: Adorno, or, the Persistence of the Dialectic*. London: Verso, 1990.

—. "On 'Cultural Studies.'" *The Ideologies of Theory*. London: Verso, 2008. 598–635.

—. *The Political Unconscious: Narrative as a Socially Symbolic Act*. Ithaca: Cornell University Press, 1981.

—. "Revisiting Postmodernism: An Interview with Fredric Jameson." *Social Text* 34.2 (June 2016): 143–160.

—. *The Seeds of Time*. New York: Columbia University Press, 1994.

—. *Valences of the Dialectic*. London: Verso, 2009.

Kipnis, Laura. "Transgression, An Elegy." *Liberties* 1 (August 2020): https://libertiesjournal.com/now-showing/transgression-an-elegy/.

Knapp, Stephen, and Walter Benn Michaels. "Against Theory." *Critical Inquiry* 8.4 (Summer 1982): 723–742.

Kornbluh, Anna. "We Have Never Been Critical: Towards the

Novel as Critique." *NOVEL* 50.3 (2017): 397–408.

Kurnick, David. "A Few Lies: Queer Theory and Our Method Melodramas." *ELH* 87.2 (Summer 2020): 349–374.

Leitch, Vincent B. *Literary Criticism in the 21st Century: Theory Renaissance*. New York: Bloomsbury, 2014.

Lentricchia, Frank. *After the New Criticism*. Chicago: University of Chicago Press, 1980.

Lesjak, Carolyn. "Reading Dialectically." *Criticism* 55.2 (2013): 233–277.

Liming, Sheila. "Fighting Words." *Los Angeles Review of Books* (December 14, 2020): https://lareviewofbooks.org/article/fighting-words/.

McNally, David. *Monsters of the Market: Zombies, Vampires, and Global Capitalism*. Chicago: Haymarket Books, 2012.

Mitchell, W. J. T. ed., *Against Theory: Literary Studies and the New Pragmatism*. Chicago: University of Chicago Press, 1985.

Moi, Toril. *Revolution of the Ordinary: Literary Studies after Wittgenstein, Austin, and Cavell*. University of Chicago Press, 2018.

Moretti, Franco, *The Bourgeois: Between History and Literature*. London: Verso, 2013.

—. ed. *Canon/Archive: Studies in Quantitative Formalism from the Stanford Literary Lab*. New York: n+1 Books, 2017.

—. *Distant Reading*. London: Verso, 2013.

—. *Graphs, Maps, Trees: Abstract Models for a Literary History*. London: Verso, 2005.

—. "Franco Moretti: A Response." *PMLA* 132.3 (May 2017): 686–689.

Nealon, Jeffrey T. *Post-Postmodernism, or the Cultural Logic of Just-in-Time Capitalism*. Palo Alto: Stanford University Press, 2012.

Olson, Gary A. *Stanley Fish, America's Enfant Terrible: The Authorized Biography*. Carbondale: Southern Illinois University Press, 2016.

Parry, Marc. "What's Wrong with Literary Studies?," *Chronicle of Higher Education* (Nov. 27, 2016): http://www.chronicle.com/article/Whats-Wrong-With-Literary/238480.

Ricoeur, Paul. *Freud and Philosophy: An Essay on Interpretation*. Trans. Denis Savage. New Haven: Yale University Press, 1970.

Robbins, Bruce. *The Beneficiary*. Durham: Duke University Press, 2017.

—. "But What About Love?" *symplokē* 28.1-2 (2020): 543–545.

—. "Critical Correctness." *The Chronicle of Higher Education* (March 12, 2019): http://www.chronicle.com/article/The-Neoliberal-Looting-of/245874 [accessed April 27, 2019].

—. "Not So Well Attached." *PMLA* 132.2 (2017): 371–376.

Robinson, Kim Stanley. *Red Mars*. New York: Bantam Books, 1993.

Said, Edward W. *Orientalism*. New York: Vintage, 1978.

—. "Traveling Theory." *The World, the Text, and the Critic*. Cambridge: Harvard University Press, 1982. 226–247.

—., *The World, the Text, and the Critic*. Cambridge: Harvard University Press, 1982.

Schuessler, Jennifer, "Reading by the Numbers: When Big Data Meets Literature," *New York Times* (October 30, 2017): https://www.nytimes.com/2017/10/30/arts/franco-moretti-stanford-literary-lab-big-data.html [accessed October 31, 2017].

Sedgwick, Eve Kosofsky. "Paranoid Reading and Reparative Reading, or, You're So Paranoid, You Probably Think This Essay Is about You." *Touching Feeling: Affect, Pedagogy, Performance*. Durham: Duke University Press, 2003. 123–152.

Tally, Robert T., Jr. "The End-of-the-World as World System." In *Other Globes: Past and Peripheral Imaginations of Globalization*. Eds. Simon Ferdinand, Irene Villaescusa-Illán, and Esther Peeren. Palgrave Macmillan, 2019. 267–283.

—. *Fredric Jameson: The Project of Dialectical Criticism*. London: Pluto, 2014.

Thompson, E. P. *The Poverty of Theory*. New York: Monthly Review Press, 1978.

Wegner, Phillip E. *Invoking Hope: Theory and Utopia in Dark Times*. Minneapolis: University of Minnesota Press, 2020.

—. Life Between Two Deaths, 1989–2001: US Culture in the Long Nineties. Durham: Duke University Press, 2009.

Williams, Jeffrey J. "The New Modesty in Literary Criticism." *The Chronicle of Higher Education* (January 5, 2015): https://www.chronicle.com/article/The-New-Modesty-in-Literary/150993.

Williams, Raymond. *Marxism and Literature*. Oxford: Oxford University Press, 1977.

Žižek, Slavoj. "The Spectre of Ideology." Introduction to *Mapping Ideology*. Ed. Slavoj Žižek. London: Verso, 1994. 1–33.

—. "We Need a Socialist Reset, Not a Corporate 'Great Reset'." *Jacobin* (December 31, 2020): https://jacobinmag.com/2020/12/slavoj-zizek-socialism-great-reset.

zer0 books

CULTURE, SOCIETY & POLITICS

The modern world is at an impasse. Disasters scroll across our smartphone screens and we're invited to like, follow or upvote, but critical thinking is harder and harder to find. Rather than connecting us in common struggle and debate, the internet has sped up and deepened a long-standing process of alienation and atomization. Zer0 Books wants to work against this trend. With critical theory as our jumping off point, we aim to publish books that make our readers uncomfortable. We want to move beyond received opinions.

Zer0 Books is on the left and wants to reinvent the left. We are sick of the injustice, the suffering and the stupidity that defines both our political and cultural world, and we aim to find a new foundation for a new struggle.

If this book has helped you to clarify an idea, solve a problem or extend your knowledge, you may want to check out our online content as well. Look for Zer0 Books: Advancing Conversations in the iTunes directory and for our Zer0 Books YouTube channel.

Popular videos include:

Žižek and the Double Blackmain
The Intellectual Dark Web is a Bad Sign
Can there be an Anti-SJW Left?
Answering Jordan Peterson on Marxism

Follow us on Facebook
at https://www.facebook.com/ZeroBooks and Twitter at https://twitter.com/Zer0Books

Bestsellers from Zer0 Books include:

Give Them An Argument
Logic for the Left
Ben Burgis
Many serious leftists have learned to distrust talk of logic. This is a serious mistake.
Paperback: 978-1-78904-210-8 ebook: 978-1-78904-211-5

Poor but Sexy
Culture Clashes in Europe East and West
Agata Pyzik
How the East stayed East and the West stayed West.
Paperback: 978-1-78099-394-2 ebook: 978-1-78099-395-9

An Anthropology of Nothing in Particular
Martin Demant Frederiksen
A journey into the social lives of meaninglessness.
Paperback: 978-1-78535-699-5 ebook: 978-1-78535-700-8

In the Dust of This Planet
Horror of Philosophy vol. 1
Eugene Thacker
In the first of a series of three books on the Horror of Philosophy, *In the Dust of This Planet* offers the genre of horror as a way of thinking about the unthinkable.
Paperback: 978-1-84694-676-9 ebook: 978-1-78099-010-1

The End of Oulipo?
An Attempt to Exhaust a Movement
Lauren Elkin, Veronica Esposito
Paperback: 978-1-78099-655-4 ebook: 978-1-78099-656-1

Capitalist Realism
Is There No Alternative?
Mark Fisher
An analysis of the ways in which capitalism has presented itself as the only realistic political-economic system.
Paperback: 978-1-84694-317-1 ebook: 978-1-78099-734-6

Rebel Rebel
Chris O'Leary
David Bowie: every single song. Everything you want to know, everything you didn't know.
Paperback: 978-1-78099-244-0 ebook: 978-1-78099-713-1

Kill All Normies
Angela Nagle
Online culture wars from 4chan and Tumblr to Trump.
Paperback: 978-1-78535-543-1 ebook: 978-1-78535-544-8

Cartographies of the Absolute
Alberto Toscano, Jeff Kinkle
An aesthetics of the economy for the twenty-first century.
Paperback: 978-1-78099-275-4 ebook: 978-1-78279-973-3

Malign Velocities
Accelerationism and Capitalism
Benjamin Noys
Long listed for the Bread and Roses Prize 2015, *Malign Velocities* argues against the need for speed, tracking acceleration as the symptom of the ongoing crises of capitalism.
Paperback: 978-1-78279-300-7 ebook: 978-1-78279-299-4

Babbling Corpse

Vaporwave and the Commodification of Ghosts

Grafton Tanner

Paperback: 978-1-78279-759-3 ebook: 978-1-78279-760-9

New Work New Culture

Work we want and a culture that strengthens us

Frithjof Bergmann

A serious alternative for mankind and the planet.

Paperback: 978-1-78904-064-7 ebook: 978-1-78904-065-4

Romeo and Juliet in Palestine

Teaching Under Occupation

Tom Sperlinger

Life in the West Bank, the nature of pedagogy and the role of a university under occupation.

Paperback: 978-1-78279-637-4 ebook: 978-1-78279-636-7

Ghosts of My Life

Writings on Depression, Hauntology and Lost Futures

Mark Fisher

Paperback: 978-1-78099-226-6 ebook: 978-1-78279-624-4

Sweetening the Pill

or How We Got Hooked on Hormonal Birth Control

Holly Grigg-Spall

Has contraception liberated or oppressed women? *Sweetening the Pill* breaks the silence on the dark side of hormonal contraception.

Paperback: 978-1-78099-607-3 ebook: 978-1-78099-608-0

Why Are We The Good Guys?

Reclaiming Your Mind from the Delusions of Propaganda

David Cromwell

A provocative challenge to the standard ideology that Western power is a benevolent force in the world.

Paperback: 978-1-78099-365-2 ebook: 978-1-78099-366-9

How to Dismantle the NHS in 10 Easy Steps (Second Edition)

Youssef El-Gingihy

The story of how your NHS was sold off and why you will have to buy private health insurance soon. A new expanded second edition with chapters on junior doctors' strikes and government blueprints for US-style healthcare.

Paperback: 978-1-78904-178-1 ebook: 978-1-78904-179-8

Digesting Recipes

The Art of Culinary Notation

Susannah Worth

A recipe is an instruction, the imperative tone of the expert, but this constraint can offer its own kind of potential. A recipe need not be a domestic trap but might instead offer escape – something to fantasise about or aspire to.

Paperback: 978-1-78279-860-6 ebook: 978-1-78279-859-0

Most titles are published in paperback and as an ebook. Paperbacks are available in traditional bookshops. Both print and ebook formats are available online.

Follow us on Facebook at https://www.facebook.com/ZeroBooks and Twitter at https://twitter.com/Zer0Books